Praise for *Teen Cyberbullying Investigated:*

"Amid all the talk about cyberbullying, Judge Jacobs's no-nonsense approach cites chapter and verse from actual court cases in a straightforward, thought-provoking way. He's not out to preach, just to inform teens, parents, and educators about the possible consequences of their actions."
—*Youth Today*

"Should be required reading for school administrators, teachers, parents, and young people when exploring the vast and still uncharted territory of the Internet."
—Ian Zack, Executive Editor, *The New York Times Upfront*

"Among books recently published on this topic, this one distinguishes itself by covering more than 50 actual court cases involving teenagers. . . . Promoting the values of civility and ethical behavior makes this book an even more timely and valuable purchase."
—*School Library Journal*

"Deals with the hot, contemporary topic of online teen harassment, by both teens and by adults. . . . Jacobs encourages readers to consider the viewpoints of victim, perpetrator, and bystander."
—*Booklist*

"Thoroughly researched and fascinating. A must-read for young people and their parents and caregivers, not just in the United States, but worldwide."
—Richard Piggin, Head of Operations, Beatbullying, London, England

"This book is at the forefront of cyberbullying literature. It has the capacity to inform school policy as parents, teachers, and principals race to find solutions for bullies and support for victims."
—Kimberley O'Brien, Principal Child Psychologist, Quirky Kid Clinic, Australia

"A great tool to provoke dialogue and help bridge the 'digital divide' between teens and adults."
—Dr. Jenny Walker, President, Cyberbullying Consulting, Ltd.

"Explains the ramifications of teen cyberbullying in a very readable format."
—Stuart Nachbar, Educated Quest blog

"A must read [that] encourages teens and educators to think about the law and what it means for those involved in cyberbullying."
—*Communiqué*, the newsletter of the National Association of School Psychologists

Teen Cyberbullying Investigated

Where Do Your Rights End and Consequences Begin?

JUDGE TOM JACOBS

Copyright © 2010 by Thomas A. Jacobs, J.D.

All rights reserved under International and Pan-American Copyright Conventions. Unless otherwise noted, no part of this book may be reproduced, stored in a retrieval system, or transmitted in any form or by any means, electronic, mechanical, photocopying, or otherwise, without express written permission of the publisher, except for brief quotations or critical reviews. For more information, go to www.freespirit.com/company/permissions.cfm.

Free Spirit, Free Spirit Publishing, and associated logos are trademarks and/or registered trademarks of Free Spirit Publishing Inc. A complete listing of our logos and trademarks is available at www.freespirit.com.

Library of Congress Cataloging-in-Publication Data
Jacobs, Thomas A.
  Teen cyberbullying investigated : where do your rights end and consequences begin? / by Tom Jacobs.
    p. cm.
  Includes bibliographical references and index.
  ISBN 978-1-57542-339-5
  1. Cyberbullying—Juvenile literature. 2. Computer crimes—Juvenile literature. 3. Technology and law—Juvenile literature. I. Title.
  HV6773.J32 2010
  345.73'025—dc22

2009043293

Free Spirit Publishing does not have control over or assume responsibility for author or third-party websites and their content. At the time of this book's publication, all facts and figures cited within are the most current available. All telephone numbers, addresses, and website URLs are accurate and active; all publications, organizations, websites, and other resources exist as described in this book; and all have been verified as of April 2014. If you find an error or believe that a resource listed here is not as described, please contact Free Spirit Publishing. Parents, teachers, and other adults: We strongly urge you to monitor children's use of the Internet.

Note: The names, ages, schools, and locations of all persons in *Teen Cyberbullying Investigated* are real, except where noted. They have been taken from public records, published court opinions, and interviews with some of those involved.

Photos on pages 14, 65, 158, 163, 164, and 166 used with permission. Page 12 © Bettman/CORBIS

Reading Level Grades 7 & Up; Interest Level Ages 12 & Up;
Fountas & Pinnell Guided Reading Level Z
Edited by Meg Bratsch
Cover and interior design by Tasha Kenyon

10 9 8 7 6 5 4
Printed in the United States of America
S18860514

Free Spirit Publishing Inc.
Minneapolis, MN
(612) 338-2068
help4kids@freespirit.com
www.freespirit.com

Free Spirit Publishing is a member of the Green Press Initiative, and we're committed to printing our books on recycled paper containing a minimum of 30% post-consumer waste (PCW). For every ton of books printed on 30% PCW recycled paper, we save 5.1 trees, 2,100 gallons of water, 114 gallons of oil, 18 pounds of air pollution, 1,230 kilowatt hours of energy, and .9 cubic yards of landfill space. At Free Spirit it's our goal to nurture not only young people, but nature too!

Free Spirit offers competitive pricing.
Contact edsales@freespirit.com for pricing information on multiple quantity purchases.

Dedication

This book is dedicated to my parents, Harry and Lucie Jacobs, for lighting and fanning the flame to read, study, and then play. It is also dedicated to Megan Meier, age 13; Rachael Neblett, age 17; Jeffrey Scott Johnston, age 15; Sam Leeson, age 13; Jessica Logan, age 18; Ryan Patrick Halligan, age 13; Holly Grogan, age 15; Megan Gillan, age 15; Hope Witsell, age 13; and all victims of cyberbullying and cyberharassment—especially those who ended their lives out of fear, frustration, and loneliness. The echo of their voices has been my inspiration.

> "A FEAR SO DEEP AND SO REAL SHE FELT HER ONLY
> WAY OUT WAS TO END HER LIFE."
> —Mark Neblett, from *A Tribute to Rachael Neblett*
> (www.makeadifferenceforkids.org)

Acknowledgments

Considering the ages of the teens featured in this book, and the writing or drawing that got them into trouble, I thought it important to note what they are doing now. My research assistant, Anne Johnson, used her Internet skills and perseverance to locate most of the featured teens. Thank you, Anne, for everything you contributed to this project. My appreciation is also extended to Susan Armstrong, Maricopa County Law Librarian, whose attention to detail kept me current throughout this endeavor. Special thanks to Natalie Jacobs, Mike Olson, Jeffrey Jacobs, Jon Davis Wiley, Ed Truman, and Parry Aftab for their insights throughout the writing of the book, and to my new Facebook and MySpace friends: Julie, Colin, Austin, Taylor, Candace, Natalia, Kali, Amy, Matt, Chase, Parker, and Alex.

Appreciation is also extended to each of you who were willing to talk with me about your case. The light you shed on your story and comments to today's youth are valuable additions to each chapter. Hopefully readers gain some insight from your experience and become better equipped to express themselves responsibly.

Once again, Free Spirit Publishing has provided me a forum to discuss an important subject. My sincere thanks go to Judy Galbraith, John Kober, Meg Bratsch, Jenni Bowring, and Tasha Kenyon for their support and professionalism throughout the creation of this book. Tasha did an outstanding job with the graphics and cover design, and my editor, Meg, worked tirelessly to polish and complete the rough manuscript I submitted. Meg, your writing and organizational skills are greatly appreciated.

And finally, my sincere appreciation to Mary Beth Tinker, Ian Zack, Emma-Jane Cross, Richard Piggin, and Kimberley O'Brien for taking time out of their busy schedules to review the book and provide their kind words.

Note Regarding Offensive Language
Some of the language in this book is, at first glance, profane and crude. It is not meant to shock, offend, or excite. Cyberbullying, by its very nature, is offensive. It is near impossible to tell these stories without the use of direct and accurate quotes from the teens involved. In the interest of free speech and presenting a meaningful study of cyberbullying, please consider any offensive language in the context for which it is presented. All quotes have been taken directly from the published opinions of the courts involved.

CONTENTS

Foreword xi

Introduction 1

PART 1: CYBERBULLYING AND THE LAW

How Did We Get Here?
The Internet and the First Amendment 8

Ethics in an e-World 16

State, Federal, and European Laws
on Cyberbullying 17

PART 2: CYBERBULLYING CASES

Chapter 1: Does Location Matter?   27
Case: *J.S. v. Bethlehem Area School District* (2002)

**Chapter 2: How a Careless Email Can
Turn Into a Federal Case**   35
Case: *Zachariah Paul v. Franklin Regional School District* (2001)

**Chapter 3: Balancing Student Rights and
School Responsibilities**   45
Case: *Justin Layshock v. Hermitage School District* (2007)

Chapter 4: Political Expression or Intentional Harassment?   53
Case: *A.B. v. State of Indiana* (2008)

**Chapter 5: When Does School Discipline
Become Unconstitutional?**   61
Case: *Avery Doninger v. Lewis Mills High School* (2008)

Chapter 6: Do Libel Laws Apply Online?   71
Case: *I.M.L. v. State of Utah* (2002)

Chapter 7: Litigating Lewdness   81
Case: *Gregory Requa v. Kent School District* (2007)

Chapter 8: What's the Issue—Content or Access? 93
Case: *Jon Coy v. Canton City Schools* (2002)

Chapter 9: Free Speech or True Threat? 101
Case: *Joshua Mahaffey v. Waterford School District* (2002)

Chapter 10: When Creative Writing Becomes Criminal Content 109
Case: *Nick Emmett v. Kent School District* (2000)

Chapter 11: When Graphic Arts Get Too Graphic 115
Case: *Aaron Wisniewski v. Weedsport Central School District* (2007)

Chapter 12: Prank or Plan? 123
Case: *State v. Joshua Mortimer* (2001)

Chapter 13: Know Thy Student Handbook 131
Case: *Jack Flaherty Jr. v. Keystone Oaks School District* (2003)

Chapter 14: Are You Responsible for Everything on Your Site? 139
Case: *Ryan Dwyer v. Oceanport School District* (2005)

Chapter 15: So You Want to Be a Hacker? 147
Case: *Justin Boucher v. School District of Greenfield* (1998)

Chapter 16: When Cyberbullying Turns Deadly 157
Case: *United States v. Lori Drew* (2008)

Closing Statement 170

How to Do Legal Research 172

Glossary of Terms 174

Additional Web Resources 182

Sources 184

Index 189

About the Author 195

Where to Get Immediate Help

If you are currently dealing with cyberbullying and need help right away, talk to a parent, teacher, counselor, or other trusted adult. Or contact one of these resources:

Wired Safety Online
www.wiredsafety.org
Click on "Getting Help" on the upper navigation menu.

BeatBullying
www.beatbullying.org
Click "I Need Help" and follow instructions to obtain help.

National Teen Dating Abuse Helpline
www.loveisrespect.org
Call 1-866-331-9474 any time or use the Web site's live chat feature. All calls and chats are anonymous and confidential.

National Sexual Assault Online Hotline
www.rainn.org
A free, confidential, secure service that provides live online help. Or call directly at 1-800-656-HOPE (1-800-656-4673).

National Suicide Prevention Hotline
www.suicide.org
Suicide is never the answer. Getting help is the answer.
Call 1-800-273-TALK (1-800-273-8255) or text: 1-800-799-4TTY (1-800-799-4889). For international hotlines, visit www.suicide.org/international-suicide-hotlines.html.

If you or someone you know is in immediate danger, **call 911.**

Foreword

The year 2009 marked the 40th anniversary of the Internet, which has done more to transform the world than any technological advance since the printing press.

The Web has revolutionized communications, turned the business world upside down (nearly killing off entire industries, like music stores, and creating new ones, like social networking sites), and enabled people everywhere instant access to dizzying amounts of information. For young people, who today often begin typing on computers and cell phones before they can read and write, the distinctions between physical space and cyberspace are increasingly melting away.

As executive editor of *The New York Times Upfront*, a national news magazine for teenagers, I've come to realize that the Web is to this generation of young people what the playground, schoolyard, and shopping mall were to mine. It's where teens (and preteens) go to explore and socialize: they surf, carry on multiple IM conversations simultaneously, and fill their Facebook pages with photos, hourly updates, and—too often—diary-like confessions.

But it's also a place where they're extremely vulnerable to attack, from complete strangers and even people they know: today's cyberbullies. I have experienced the old-fashioned kind of bullying. As a fifth grader, I was tormented for almost a year by a boy who smacked me and challenged me to hit him back (I refused) until he lost interest and found other prey.

Those schoolyard bullies still exist, of course, but cyberbullying can be just as terrifying, though in a very different way: The aggression is carried out online, with victims subjected to harassment or public ridicule. And thanks to the viral nature of the Web, the audience can be virtually limitless.

According to the *Journal of Adolescent Health*, between a tenth and a third of young people have been victimized by a cyberbully, and schools around the nation are scrambling to create policies to deal with the phenomenon. Not surprisingly, as with most things related to the Web, the law is still playing catch up when it comes to figuring out how to handle cyberbullying. But it IS beginning to catch up.

That's why Judge Jacobs's book is so valuable. Using real court cases and stories of both cyberbullies and their victims, he provides a road map to the current state of the law regarding online harassment. In addition, he offers practical advice on how to make sure your own online communications—including private emails and texts—don't get you into trouble.

It should be required reading not only for victims of this 21st century form of bullying, but also for school administrators, teachers, parents, and young people who need to have their wits about them when they're exploring the vast and still uncharted territory of the Internet.

Ian Zack
Executive Editor
The New York Times Upfront

Introduction

Technology is likely part of your natural environment as a teen today. You were born into a technology-rich "wired" world, heavily influenced by the Internet. Consider these statistics:

> "THE INTERNET IS ALWAYS A WILLING LISTENER, ANY TIME OF THE DAY OR NIGHT."
> —Rachel Dretzin, "Growing Up Online," *PBS Frontline*, 2008

- 16 million children ages 2 to 11 were online in May 2009. The 2- to 4-year-olds were exposed to the Internet while on their parents' laps in front of a computer.
- Among 12- to 14-year-olds in the United States, 88% use the Internet. This figure trails Great Britain (100%), Israel (98%), and the Czech Republic (96%).
- More than 90% of teens are online and more than half of them have profiles on social networking sites.
- 85% of teens communicate through digital writing.
- 85% of high school students spend at least one hour daily on the Internet.

This Web-based culture has resulted in exciting new ways to communicate, learn, socialize, stay informed, entertain yourself, and foster your creativity. However, it has also presented new challenges for you and your friends that were not faced by your parents or grandparents, or perhaps even by your older siblings. For example, you may be asking yourself daily questions such as:

"Are there limits to what I can do once I'm online?"

"How do I know who sees information once I post it on a Web site?"

- France has made access to the Internet a "human right."
- Internet access is a "legal right" in Finland as of July 2010.
- In 2009, Uruguay became the first Latin American country to provide every student in public elementary school with a computer through The One Laptop Per Child program.

"Can I share my feelings online about others—my classmates, teachers, or principal—without getting into trouble?"

"Can my school discipline me for what I do on my cell phone or my home computer?"

"Are there things I should never post or send online?"

The growth of the Internet has added a new complexity to issues regarding your free expression as a student—both on and off school grounds. And in addition to opening up positive new ways to communicate, it has also given rise to endless new ways to threaten, harass, abuse, insult, and bully others. Gone are the days when bullying meant a shove in the hallway or an insult yelled across a classroom. Bullying has entered the digital age. With the click of a button or touch of a screen, a photo, video, or conversation can be shared with a few people in an email or text . . . or broadcast to millions on a Web site. Pictures and messages that used to be scribbled on paper and passed in class are now posted online.

Have you ever received a hurtful email, text, or instant message? Has someone made cruel comments about you on an online profile or blog? Has someone taken a picture or video of you at school or outside of school and posted it on a Web site like YouTube, MySpace, or Facebook? Have you sent what you thought was a personal message to a friend and later found out it's all over your school? And finally, have you ever done any of these to someone else? If you answered, "yes" to any of these questions, you've been involved in *cyberbullying*.

> **A New Breed of Bully**
>
> In Singapore, a 16-year-old girl created fake profiles on MySpace and Facebook in order to befriend kids she didn't like at school. Once she connected with the kids, she turned on them with nasty insults. "The new breed of bullies is narcissistic (self-centered). They treat the Internet as their stage, with an instant audience of thousands—or even millions," said Dr. Carol Balhetchet of Singapore Children's Society.

Most cyberbullying involving kids and teens is done by their peers and occurs as early as 2nd grade. Cyberbullying takes many forms, with the most common being:

- sending insulting or threatening emails, texts, or instant messages directly to someone using a computer, cell phone, or other e-communication device
- spreading hateful comments about someone through emails, blogs, online profiles, or chat rooms
- stealing passwords and sending out threatening messages using a false identity
- building a Web site targeting specific people

> 85% of middle school children report being cyberbullied at least once.
>
> 32% of American teens who use the Internet report some form of online harassment.
>
> In a recent study, 72% of participants, ages 12 to 17, claimed they knew who was doing the cyberbullying.

> "KIDS DON'T KNOW HOW COMMON CYBERBULLYING IS, EVEN AMONG THEIR BEST FRIENDS."
> —Professor Jaana Juvonen, Developmental Psychology Program Chair, UCLA

This book provides an inside, in-depth look at the current cyberbullying epidemic. Presented here are real cases of tweens and teens who were harassed or caught harassing others online, on camera, in a text, or using a cell phone. Some cases were harmless pranks or creative musings, while others caused serious emotional and physical injury to others. Your teachers, school administrators, and parents may be up to their ears in information about monitoring your use of the Internet and cell phones.

It's time for *you* to know about what's happening to your peers, learn what your legal rights are, and decide for yourself how you will use these devices for your benefit.

Most of the teens discussed in this book engaged in cyberbullying behavior, whether their target was another person or the school in general. And each of the teens paid a price, even those who eventually won their cases in court. Many served suspension days; others were hospitalized for evaluation or screened by a doctor or psychologist; some were banned from sports or other activities; and a few were expelled from school or jailed. In some manner, each teen and his or her family were adversely affected due to consequences at school, police involvement, legal proceedings, and, in a few cases, needing to relocate to another city.

In addition to perpetrators, several victims of cyberbullying are also discussed here, including Megan Meier, Rachael Neblett, Jessica Logan, Sam Leeson, Holly Grogan, Megan Gillan, Jeffrey Johnston, and Ryan Patrick Halligan. For these teens, experiences of being bullied online led to devastating ends. The Internet is a modern wonder with unlimited potential . . . but if abused it can also wreak havoc on individuals,

> It's now more important than ever for you to **think before you click.**

One Teen's Comments About the Internet

To be a teen is to be in the process of creating the adult you will one day become. Every new thing you are exposed to might be compared to a seed that, depending on whether it's one of the few that you choose to cultivate, may blossom in your adulthood.

Until very recently, these "seeds" were provided only by a teen's direct surroundings and the relatively limited and pre-selected things found in books and magazines, and on the radio and television. However, teens today have found a channel through which they can expose themselves to almost anything with just a click of a mouse. The Internet has changed our world immeasurably, affecting us socially and psychologically probably more than any other invention, and propelling us into a new age driven entirely by information.

With the aid of the Internet, we can observe the world as we might observe something through a glass wall, and though this cannot even begin to compare to learning about and experiencing things directly, seeing something through a families, schools, and communities. Virtual-world speech often carries real-world consequences.

Attempts were made to personally interview each of the teens whose cases are presented in this book. Their thoughts and comments are reported in the "What Is ____ Doing Now?" section of each chapter. Thanks to all who contributed to this endeavor, and good luck in your current pursuits.

I'm always interested in hearing from teens about their experiences and questions. If you'd like to get in touch with me, you can contact me in care of:

Free Spirit Publishing
217 Fifth Avenue North, Suite 200
Minneapolis, MN 55401-1299

Or you can email me at help4kids@freespirit.com

I look forward to hearing from you!

Tom Jacobs, J.D.

---

glass wall is better than not seeing it at all. In this way, teens today are able to endow themselves with many more "seeds" than those of previous generations could have imagined.

The result—scary to some and inspiring to others—is that it's easier than ever for kids to grow into an adult that is entirely different from the people among whom they were brought up. Growing up has never been devoid of bad influences, and the fact is that most teens slip up some time in their lives—whether they grew up in the 21st century or in the 1st. As the saying goes: "With freedom comes responsibility." Part of being a teen is learning to have the responsibility to make the right decisions.

The Internet, like the world it imitates, is full of terrible and fantastic things, allowing young people more freedom than ever to choose who they will become, and, essentially, redefining what it is to be a teenager.

—Theodora Ballew, freshman at North High School, Phoenix, Arizona, 2008

Part 1
Cyberbullying and the Law

How Did We Get Here?
The Internet and the First Amendment

Central to any discussion of cyberbullying is a document that was composed in 1789: the First Amendment to the U.S. Constitution.

> Congress shall make no law respecting an establishment of religion, or prohibiting the free exercise thereof; **or abridging the freedom of speech,** or of the press; or the right of the people peaceably to assemble, and to petition the Government for a redress of grievances.
> —The First Amendment of the U.S. Constitution, ratified in 1791

In 1997, the United States Supreme Court stated that the Internet is protected by the First Amendment. This does not mean, however, that you can say anything you like about anyone without consequences. The First Amendment provides protection for speech that is *reasonable under the circumstances*. For example, you can't stand up in a crowded theater and, as a joke, yell "Fire!" without getting into trouble. Likewise, you can't post a threat online about hurting your teachers or classmates without facing examination, and, possibly, serious consequences.

The horrific events at Columbine High School in Colorado in 1999 remain fresh in the world's mind—when two students brought guns to school and killed 12 students, a teacher, and themselves, after posting threats of violence online. Since then, tension has grown between student free speech, particularly online speech, and school safety. Even so, as you will see in the cases discussed here, courts strive to interpret and apply the First Amendment as our Founding Fathers intended.

To ensure that your First Amendment freedoms are guaranteed in the fast-growing medium of cyberspace, the law must keep pace with the Internet. As a student today, you likely spend quite a bit of time exercising your First Amendment rights online—emailing, IMing, blogging, texting, sharing photos, posting material on social networking sites, and so on—both in school and out. So it is important for you to know how law enforcement and the courts view these activities. As you read these cases, you'll see the evolution of legal protection to ever-changing technologies, and the ongoing attempts to balance free speech rights of students with the responsibilities of schools. Keep in mind that a court's decision affects only those within its jurisdiction. Although a court's ruling may be persuasive, it may not apply in your state.

> **Unsure what a word means?** Some of the legal and Internet-related terms used in this book might be unfamiliar to you. Check the glossary on pages 174–181 for definitions.

U.S. Court System At-a-Glance*

	State Court—civil and criminal cases involving state and local laws	**Federal Court**—cases involving the U.S. Constitution and its Amendments, or laws passed by Congress
Trial Court—cases presented before a judge or jury	**State Trial Courts** Juvenile Court Municipal Court Justice Court Traffic Court Police Court Superior Court	**Federal Trial Courts** U.S. District Court
Appellate Court—trial court decisions may be appealed and sent to higher appellate courts	**State Appellate Courts** Court of Appeals State Supreme Court	**Federal Appellate Courts** U.S. Circuit Court U.S. Supreme Court

* The names of each level of court may vary by state.

THE RIGHTS OF MINORS

You may be wondering how the courts became involved with your personal expression in the first place. It wasn't that long ago that children and teens had no standing under the law. Kids were considered the property of their parents with no recognized individual rights.

In 1899, the country's first juvenile court was created in Chicago, Illinois, to deal with delinquent children. However, the question of student free expression received little attention until years later. In one of the earliest cases involving a minor, the Supreme Court of Wisconsin ruled in 1908 that school officials had the power to suspend two high school girls, Hazel and Mabel Dresser, for writing a "harmless" poem that ridiculed the school rules and was printed in a local paper. The girls' prank occurred off-campus and not at a school event or while they were under the control of the principal. Sixty years before the famous *Tinker* case (see next page), the court ruled that "school authorities have the power to suspend a pupil for an offense committed outside of school hours which has a tendency to influence the conduct of other pupils, to set at naught the proper discipline of the school, impair the authority of the teachers, and bring them into ridicule and contempt." The court said, "Such power is essential to the preservation of order, decency, decorum, and good government in the public schools."*

> **Rules of the St. Croix Jail**
>
> You must shut your mouth at noontime,
> You must shut it at recess,
> You must keep it shut at morning,
> And all other times, I guess.
>
> When you get up to leave the room,
> Don't take a friend along;
> You must not once quit working hard,
> Because you know that's wrong.
>
> Can't even stop to tie your shoe,
> To blow your nose or cough,
> Don't look up from your book at all,
> And don't you dare to laugh.
>
> Just calmly wait 'til four o'clock,
> You know that comes 'round soon,
> And then you're free from prison,
> Until the next forenoon.
>
> —Hazel and Mabel Dresser, Wisconsin, 1906

---
* The suspension would end when the girls apologized and each paid the school a 40-cent fine.

The U.S. Supreme Court (a.k.a. "the Court") exerts a powerful influence over the course of the nation and over the lives of all Americans—including students. It was not long before the Court weighed in on the matter of student free expression, and the judicial system began to recognize its role in education as more complex. In 1940, Supreme Court Justice Felix Frankfurter said, "The courtroom is not the arena for debating issues of educational policy." In 1943, the Supreme Court decided that under the First Amendment, public school students may refuse to salute the flag or say the Pledge of Allegiance. The Court wrote that it must ensure "scrupulous protection of constitutional freedoms of the individual," including the rights of children. "We can have intellectual individualism and the rich cultural diversities that we owe to exceptional minds only at the price of occasional eccentricity and abnormal attitudes."

Then, in the landmark 1967 case known as *In re Gault*, which concerned the arrest of a 15-year-old boy in Arizona, the Court ruled that teenagers have distinct rights under the U.S. Constitution. *Gault* only involved the rights of minors who were arrested and charged with a crime, but it opened the door for courts to further expand the rights of minors.

Tinker and Student Expression

Two years after *In re Gault*, the door opened wide when the Supreme Court decided the famous *Tinker* case. In 1965, the four Tinker children (John, Mary Beth, Paul, and Hope) and their friend Chris Eckhardt decided to express their opposition to the Vietnam War by wearing black armbands to school in Des Moines, Iowa.

This violated school policy and the students were sent home until they removed the armbands. In 1969, the Supreme Court ruled in their favor in what has become the *Tinker* standard for school censorship of student expression. Public school

> "WE NEED TO ENCOURAGE OUR YOUTH TO ENGAGE IN CONTROVERSY, NOT DISENGAGE FROM IT."
> —John Tinker, commenting in 2009

> "I RECOMMEND INVIGORATING THE FIRST AMENDMENT BY USING IT. TEENS WITH THEIR CREATIVITY, CURIOSITY, AND, TO SOME, OUTRAGEOUS SENSE OF HUMOR, ARE NATURALS WHEN IT COMES TO HOLDING THE FIRST AMENDMENT TO THE TEST OF TIME, EVEN IN THESE TIMES."
> —Mary Beth Tinker, commenting in 2009

Mary Beth and John Tinker with their armbands

> "IT CAN HARDLY BE ARGUED THAT EITHER STUDENTS OR TEACHERS SHED THEIR CONSTITUTIONAL RIGHTS TO FREEDOM OF SPEECH OR EXPRESSION AT THE SCHOOLHOUSE GATE."
>
> "STUDENTS IN SCHOOL AS WELL AS OUT OF SCHOOL ARE 'PERSONS' UNDER OUR CONSTITUTION."
> —both quotes from the *Tinker* decision

officials must tolerate student speech as long as it does not materially or substantially disrupt the educational environment or invade the rights of others to be secure.

The challenge today for schools and courts is applying the *Tinker* test to digital expression, which has become an essential part of kids' lives. The *Tinker* court recognized that "personal intercommunication among the students is an important part of the educational process."

Fraser and Offensive Speech

In a 1975 case, the Supreme Court affirmed the *Tinker* decision, stating, "[T]he system of public education that has evolved in this Nation relies necessarily upon the discretion and judgment of school administrators and school board members, and we are not authorized to intervene absent violations of specific constitutional guarantees." However, a little over a decade later, in the 1986 *Fraser* case, the Court

> **Public Schools v. Private Schools**
> Be aware that the cases presented in this book regard public school students only. Generally, private schools are not required to recognize free speech or free press protections of student expression. "State action" (i.e., government involvement) is what triggers the First Amendment. These cases don't apply to the private school student, unless your state has a law protecting private school students from First Amendment violations, such as California's Leonard Law (Calif. Educ. Code 48950).

addressed student expression again. This time, however, it did intervene, ruling against lewd and plainly offensive speech at school.

Matthew Fraser was a junior at Bethel High School in Washington. He gave a nominating speech for a fellow classmate before a student assembly. Matthew admitted that he deliberately used sexual metaphors and was suspended from school for three days. The Court upheld his suspension reasoning that "a high school assembly or classroom is no place for a sexually explicit monologue directed towards an unsuspecting audience of teenage students. . . . Public schools may prohibit the use of vulgar and offensive terms in public discourse."

> "THE UNDOUBTED FREEDOM TO ADVOCATE UNPOPULAR, CONTROVERSIAL VIEWS IN SCHOOLS AND CLASSROOMS MUST BE BALANCED AGAINST THE SOCIETY'S COUNTERVAILING INTEREST IN TEACHING STUDENTS THE BOUNDARIES OF SOCIALLY APPROPRIATE BEHAVIOR."
> —from the *Fraser* decision

Hazelwood and School Censorship

Shortly after *Fraser*, in 1988, the Court again narrowed the *Tinker* standard in a case involving written expression. The principal of Hazelwood High School in Missouri censored two stories in the school newspaper written by students in the journalism class. The articles dealt with the impact of teen pregnancy and divorce on teenagers, topics that were considered hot button issues by the school and deemed inappropriate for inclusion in a student publication. The Supreme Court agreed with the school's action, holding that "Educators do not offend the First Amendment by exercising editorial control over the style and content of student speech in school-sponsored expressive activities" so long as their actions are reasonably related to the school's mission.

Frederick and Illegal Activity

The principles of *Hazelwood* were extended in a 2007 Supreme Court decision involving a senior at Juneau-Douglas High School in Alaska. Joseph Frederick was suspended for 10 days for displaying a banner at a school

> "THE EDUCATION OF THE NATION'S YOUTH IS PRIMARILY THE RESPONSIBILITY OF PARENTS, TEACHERS, AND STATE AND LOCAL OFFICIALS, AND NOT OF FEDERAL JUDGES."
> —from the *Hazelwood* decision.

> "IT IS THE INDIVIDUAL'S RESPONSIBILITY TO MAKE SURE WHAT THEY ARE SAYING IS LEGITIMATE AND CAN BE BACKED UP AND DOES NOT HARM ANOTHER."
> —Cathy Kuhlmeier, one of the Hazelwood student journalists, commenting in 2009

Joseph Frederick and classmates displaying banner (photo courtesy of Clay Good)

> Commenting in 2009, Joseph Frederick, then teaching in China, said he's careful about what he puts online. "There's no real privacy on the Internet."

event that read, "Bong Hits 4 Jesus." His message was not protected speech since the Court ruled that school officials could censor speech that was "reasonably viewed as promoting illegal drug use." An interesting comment in that case came from Justice Clarence Thomas who argued that public school students should have no free speech rights whatsoever. He stated, "In my view, the history of public education suggests that the First Amendment, as originally understood, does not protect student speech in public schools."

THE LIMITS OF STUDENT SPEECH ARE STILL PENDING

You see from this history that you have First Amendment rights at school, but they are restricted—and often the cause of heated controversy. The Supreme Court has yet to decide the official limits of student Internet speech or the ramifications of cell phone use at school, text messaging, and other electronic forms of communication. But as you'll read in the cases that follow, it won't be long before these issues reach the highest court. The Supreme Court did state in 1997 that speech on the Internet is entitled to the highest level of protection. However, the Court in that case was not speaking about minors and the extent of protection remains undecided. As Avery Doninger (see chapter 5) wrote in a 2008 essay regarding her case, "Eventually, the scales of justice will determine whether students have speech rights off campus in the age of the Internet and whether there is a difference between 'shouldn't have said' and 'didn't have the right to say.'"

> "OFF-CAMPUS SPEECH CAN BECOME ON-CAMPUS SPEECH WITH THE CLICK OF A MOUSE."
> —Doninger v. Niehoff, U.S. District Court (2009)

The First Amendment is alive and well in the United States, thanks to responsible schools and educators, and the pioneering students and parents willing to take a stand on these developing issues. Keep the *Tinker, Fraser, Hazelwood,* and *Frederick* cases in mind and what the court said in each as you read further.

> "FREE SPEECH NOT ONLY LIVES, IT ROCKS!"
> —Oprah Winfrey

Ethics in an e-World

Along with legal issues involving free speech on the Internet come ethical questions to think about. Consider the following scenario as an example.

Imagine it's Friday night and you're at a party at a friend's house. Everyone there is 15 or 16 and your friend's parents are keeping a low profile. Someone sneaks in alcohol. You take a few pictures of people drinking and post them on your MySpace page the next day. Your school principal sees the pictures and disciplines the students identified in them for underage drinking. Some are suspended for a few days, while others are restricted from participating in their extracurricular activities.

What is your ethical responsibility, if any, in this situation? As one of the kids at the party, did you respect your friends' privacy by sharing the photos with the world? Did you think that only your immediate circle of friends would view the photos? Sometimes well-intentioned acts result in significant unintended harms.

Anyone with an Internet connection can be a reporter, critic, commentator, or media producer. It is no longer just you and a few friends or family members. Uploading videos to YouTube, instant messaging, or writing blog entries enables you to be a socially responsible participant in cyberspace. The potential for irresponsible choices exists, too, such as violating the rights of others, or in the extreme, becoming a cyberbully.

Whether you're blogging, emailing, or playing an online game, your audience in cyberspace is vast and unknowable.

What does it mean to be a good citizen in our e-world? Do you have any responsibility when communicating via digital media? Are you concerned about how you portray yourself to others? What about protecting your privacy and respecting the privacy of others? Have you thought about the implications of cyberbullying, or downloading sexually suggestive photos, or faking your personal profile to fool others? Think about these ethical issues while reading the cases in this book. If these teens had considered questions of cyberethics, might they have acted differently?

State, Federal, and European Laws on Cyberbullying

The cyberbullying epidemic has the attention of state legislatures, the federal government, and countries across the globe. Cities and towns are also addressing the problem by passing laws about electronic harassment. Following are some of the existing federal and state laws dealing with this public health issue.

Many of the laws require public schools to develop policies prohibiting cyberbullying and cyberharassment. Some of the laws authorize discipline ranging from suspension to expulsion, and a few also address off-campus activities that affect the school environment. Other laws require reporting incidents of bullying to law enforcement officials. Expect to see more cities, states, and countries getting onboard with their own laws in the near future.

There are several ways you can locate and read the specific laws for yourself. Since laws can be modified or repealed, check the currency of the law if you plan to cite it in research.

- Google the name of the law or act. Include the name of the state if it's a state law.
- Google the number of the law with the name of the state. (See the list of state laws on pages 18–21. Numbers are included in brackets following each law.)
- Ask a parent or librarian for help.

FEDERAL LAWS

The **Megan Meier Cyberbullying Prevention Act** was first introduced in the U.S. Congress in May 2008. Passage by the House and Senate and signing by the President is pending. You can follow the bill's progress (House Resolution 1966) by logging on to www.govtrack.us, a Web site that follows all legislation introduced in Congress. Type in "Megan Meier" and search for the latest version of the bill. Read about Megan's case in chapter 16, pages 157–169.

In 2008, Congress passed the **Protecting Children in the 21st Century Act** (also known as the Broadband Data Improvement Act). It requires public schools to educate their students about cyberbullying, online safety, and sexual predators. It also calls for the Federal Trade Commission to conduct a national public-awareness campaign about these issues.

The **Communications Decency Act** (1996) protects online users and service providers from legal action against them for the comments of others. See Ryan Dwyer's case in chapter 14 (pages 139–145) for an example.

The **Interstate Communications Law** (1948) makes it a felony to communicate across state lines a threat to kidnap, extort, or injure another person.

STATE LAWS

Arkansas: "Bullying" includes electronic communications that cause physical harm to a student or teacher, or substantial disruption at school. The law also allows for action against some off-campus activities. [Sec. 6-18-514]

California: A student may be suspended or expelled for cyberbullying by text, sound, image, or message by means of an electronic device during school hours or at a school-related activity. Electronic

> A 2008 state law in California requires foster parents and staff members at group homes for foster children to receive training about laws to protect students from bullying on campus.

devices include mobile phones, computers, pagers, and any wireless device. [Education Code Secs. 32261 and 48900]

Colorado: School districts are required to provide an Internet Safety Plan in grades K–12 for "recognition and avoidance of online bullying." [Sec. 22-32-109.1]

Delaware: The School Bullying Prevention Act (2007) authorizes action against off-campus cyberbullying that affects the school environment. [Title 14 Sec. 4112D]

Florida: The Jeffrey Johnston Stand Up for All Students Act (2008) includes discipline for off-campus cyberbullying if it affects a student's performance or disrupts the school. [Sec. 1006.147]

Idaho: Students may be suspended for bullying others using a telephone or computer and such an act constitutes a crime of harassment. [Secs. 18-917A (2006) and 33-205]

Illinois: The Internet Safety Education Act (2008) requires all public school districts to teach Internet safety courses to grades 3 and above. It also adds electronic communications to the harassment laws, including the creation of a Web site or page for the purpose of bullying someone. [Sec. 720 ILCS 135/1-2]

Iowa: Schools must create policies prohibiting harassment and bullying in school and at any school function or school sponsored activity. [Sec. 280.28 (2007)]

Kansas: Cyberbullying includes threats by any electronic communication device including but not limited to email, instant message, text message, blogs, mobile phones, pagers, online games, and Web sites. [KSA Sec. 72-8256 (2008)]

Kentucky: The Golden Rule Act (2008) prohibits written harassment and other forms of intimidation, and states that harassment includes substantially disrupting a school and creating a hostile environment at school. [Sec. 525.070]

Maryland: School administrators may report off-campus cyberbullying and other forms of intimidation if it disrupts the orderly operation of the school. [Sec. 7-424]

Minnesota: Requires schools to create written policies prohibiting intimidation and bullying of any student, including through use of the Internet. [Sec. 121A.0695 (2007)]

Missouri: Harassment by computer, text message, and other electronic devices is illegal; it is a felony for an adult (age 21 or older) to cyberbully anyone 17 or younger. [Sec. 565.090 (2008)]

> Following the suicide of 13-year-old Megan Meier in 2006 (see chapter 16, pages 157–169), the city of Dardenne Prairie, Missouri, passed a measure outlawing online harassment. Violation of the law is a misdemeanor punishable by a $500 fine and 90 days in jail.

Nebraska: Bullying includes electronic abuse on school grounds or at school events and may result in long-term suspension, expulsion, or reassignment. [NRS Secs. 79-2, 137 and 79-267 (2008)]

New Jersey: Electronic communication is added to the definition of bullying, and schools may discipline when acts disrupt school. [Sec. 18A:37-14 (2007)]

> In 2008, New Jersey became one of the first states to address a cyberbullying policy for college and university students.

Oklahoma: The School Bullying Prevention Act (2008) states that bullying, harassment, and intimidation covers electronic communication by any means including telephone, cell phone, computer, or other wireless device that disrupts or interferes with a student's education. [Sec. 70 Sec. 24-100.3]

Oregon: Cyberbullying is added to the definition of bullying, which is prohibited at school or "immediately adjacent to school grounds or at school sponsored activities." [Sec. 339.351 (2007)]

Pennsylvania: Harassment and stalking may be committed through electronic means, phone, email, the Internet, or wireless communication. [Pa. C.S.A. 18 Secs. 2709 and 2709.1 (2008)]

Rhode Island: Harassment includes any act of electronic communication including any verbal, graphic, or textual communication by any electronic device. A first offense is a misdemeanor and a second is a felony. [Sec. 16-21-26 (2008)]

South Carolina: The Safe School Climate Act allows schools to discipline cyberbullies. Electronic communications are included in the definition of bullying. [Sec. 59-63-120 (2006)]

Washington: Added electronic harassment to the state's bullying laws, requiring schools to implement prevention policies. [Sec. 28A-300.285 (2007)]

EUROPE'S RESPONSE TO CYBERBULLYING

The 27 countries of the European Union agreed in 2008 to spend $70 million to make the Internet safer for children and teens. Over 12,000 parents across Europe were surveyed and their concerns about online bullying and sexual harassment prompted the agreement.

In 2009, the European Union signed a pact with 17 social networking sites to curb the growing trend of cyberbullying. The agreement requires the sites, which include MySpace, Facebook, Bebo, Yahoo! Europe, Skyrock, and YouTube, to ensure the profiles of users under age 18 are set to "private," and they cannot be found through other Web sites or search engines. It also requires the sites to provide a one-click button for reporting abuse or unwanted contact.

> The European Union has declared one day each February **International Safer Internet Day.** For more information go to www.saferinternet.org.

Part 1: Further Reading and Resources

Berlin, Seth D., and Sinclair Stafford. "Teach Your Children: High School Students and the First Amendment." *Communications Lawyer* 25, no. 4 (July 2008): 13.

Billitteri, Thomas J. "Cyberbullying: Are New Laws Needed to Curb Online Aggression?" *Congressional Quarterly Researcher* 18, no. 17 (2008): 385–408.

C-Span • www.c-spanarchives.org/library (Click "Search" and enter the Program ID "283995-1")
C-Span's *America and the Courts* program highlights the 40th anniversary of *Tinker v. Des Moines Independent Community School District.* This includes interviews with Mary Beth Tinker and Joseph Frederick from the "Bong Hits 4 Jesus" case.

"Cyberbullying Europe—How Is Europe Dealing With It?" by the European Commission (Feb. 16, 2009) at: www.egovmonitor.com/node/23450

David-Ferdon, Corinne, and Marci Feldman Hertz. "Electronic Media, Violence, and Adolescents: An Emerging Public Health Problem." *Journal of Adolescent Health* 41, no. 6 (December 2007): 1–5.

Kosse, Susan Hanley, and Robert H. Wright. "How Best to Confront the Bully: Should Title IX or Antibullying Statutes Be the Answer." *Duke Journal of Gender Law & Policy* 12 (Spring 2005): 53.

Dunton Lam, Anne. "Student Threats and the First Amendment." Institute of Government, University of North Carolina at Chapel Hill, *School Law Bulletin* 33, no. 2 (Spring 2002): 1–12.

Erb, Todd D. "A Case for Strengthening School District Jurisdiction to Punish Off-Campus Incidents of Cyberbullying." *Arizona State Law Journal* 40, no. 1 (Spring 2008): 257.

Garnett, Richard W. "Can There Really Be 'Free Speech' in Public Schools?" *Lewis & Clark Law Review* 12, no. 1 (2008): 45–59.

Gold Waldman, Emily. "Student Speech Rights: The State of the Law Post–*Morse v. Frederick*." Lecture, Eighth Annual School Law Institute, New York, NY, May 19, 2008.

Strossen, Nadine. "Keeping the Constitution Inside the Schoolhouse Gates: Students' Rights Thirty Years After *Tinker v. Des Moines Independent Community School District*." *Drake University Law Review* 48, no. 3 (2000): 445–462.

Swartz, Jennifer Kathleen. "Beyond the Schoolhouse Gates: Do Students Shed Their Constitutional Rights When Communicating to a Cyber-Audience?" *Drake Law Review* 48, no. 3 (2000): 587.

Verga, Rita J. "Policing Their Space: The First Amendment Parameters of School Discipline of Student Cyberspeech." *Santa Clara Computer & High Technology Law Journal* 23, no. 4 (2007): 727–748.

Part 2
Cyberbullying Cases

CHAPTER 1

Does Location Matter?

Case: *J.S. v. Bethlehem Area School District (2002)*

Act: creating a Web site with personal attacks against school faculty members

Charge: threatening physical harm to a teacher and principal

Welcome To Teacher Sux

Disclaimer: By clicking Agree, you agree to all of the following:

1. I will not give up the identity of the person who runs this site and/or any person(s) who have help build it.
2. I will not tell any employees of the Bethlehem Area School District staff about this site.
3. I waive my right to persecute or prosecute any person due to the data on the following pages.
4. I do not work for the Bethlehem Area School District staff.
5. I believe in the freedom of speech.
6. I have no intentions of getting the owner in trouble.
7. I will not print any material found on this site and then show it to a staff member of the BASD.
8. I will not in any way show this site to any staff members of the Bethlehem Area School District.
9. If I disobey any of the agreements, I am going in this site illegally and aware that I may be prosecuted.

| Agree | I do not agree with 1 or more of the rules. |

Justin Swidler was 14 and in 8th grade at Nitschman Middle School in Pennsylvania. Justin was upset with his algebra teacher, Kathleen Fulmer, and the principal, Thomas Kartsotis, and they became the targets of his frustration. He designed and wrote a Web site named "Teacher Sux" in 1998.

A few pages dedicated to Ms. Fulmer consisted of degrading comments and personal attacks, such as this statement, repeated 136 times: *"Fuck You Mrs. Fulmer. You Are A Bitch. You Are A Stupid Bitch."* A picture of her face morphing into Adolf Hitler was accompanied by the caption, "Why she should die," and the statement, "Take a look at the diagram and the reasons I gave, then give me $20 to help pay for the hit man." A drawing of her with her head cut off and blood dripping from her neck was posted with the statement, "We all wish this would happen." In addition, Justin posted a picture of the principal morphing into a clown, along with sexual comments and personal attacks.

Principal Kartsotis took the threats seriously and called the police. The FBI became involved, too, but no charges were brought against Justin. During the investigation, Justin voluntarily closed down the Web site.

The school held expulsion hearings. They learned that Ms. Fulmer, who had been teaching for 26 years, was afraid that someone would try to kill her. She suffered from stress, anxiety, and loss of sleep, appetite, and weight. She was unable to finish the semester and took a medical leave for the next year. The school district voted to permanently expel Justin from its schools for threats against a teacher and the principal, and the physical harm to Ms. Fulmer.

Justin and his parents appealed the school's decision, and the case went to court. He and his parents claimed there wasn't a sufficient disruption at school to limit Justin's off-campus speech. They also argued that his Web site did not contain a true threat to anyone. The school asserted that although created at Justin's home, the Web site affected school personnel and, in fact, *did* constitute a threat to Ms. Fulmer.

HOW WOULD YOU DECIDE THIS CASE?

Are you surprised that Justin's school district expelled him for something he did at home? What do you think was the last straw that resulted in his expulsion—the comparison to Hitler, the crude language, the sexual comments, or the solicitation of a hit man? What about the effect Justin had on Ms. Fulmer's health, does that matter? If you saw yourself depicted on someone's Web site the way Justin depicted Ms. Fulmer, would you feel threatened or fearful?

WHAT THE COURT DECIDED

In court, the school had to prove that Justin's Web site constituted a *true threat*, in which case it would not be protected speech and they could punish him. If it was not a true threat, the school could still expel Justin if they proved that his actions disrupted the school environment. The court concluded that, although crude and highly offensive, Justin's statements did not constitute a true threat. The site "did not reflect a serious expression of intent to inflict harm." However, the court decided that the site *was* disruptive at school.

True, Justin created his Web site off-campus (away from school grounds). He also included the disclaimer about not showing the site to any school staff members. However, the disclaimer offered no legal protection for Justin, and the court ruled that there was a sufficient connection with the school to consider the site's content to be on-campus speech. "Teacher

> "IN THIS DAY AND AGE WHERE SCHOOL VIOLENCE IS BECOMING MORE COMMONPLACE, SCHOOL OFFICIALS ARE JUSTIFIED IN TAKING THREATS AGAINST FACULTY AND STUDENTS SERIOUSLY."
>
> "THE ADVENT OF THE INTERNET HAS COMPLICATED ANALYSIS OF RESTRICTIONS ON SPEECH. ... TINKER'S SIMPLE ARMBAND WORN SILENTLY AND BROUGHT INTO A DES MOINES, IOWA, CLASSROOM, HAS BEEN REPLACED BY JUSTIN SWIDLER'S COMPLEX, MULTIMEDIA WEB SITE, ACCESSIBLE TO FELLOW STUDENTS, TEACHERS, AND THE WORLD."
>
> —Both quotes from Justin Swidler's case

Sux" was clearly aimed at a specific audience: Justin's fellow students and the school community. Justin also mentioned his site in class and showed it to another student.

The court claimed the physical and mental harm to Ms. Fulmer, the need for substitute teachers to cover her classes, and the impact on the student body all contributed to disorder and substantial interference with the work of the school. Justin's First Amendment claim was denied. His permanent expulsion was affirmed.

In addition, Ms. Fulmer and Principal Kartsotis sued Justin and his family for violating their civil rights. A jury ruled in favor of Ms. Fulmer, awarding her $450,000 for invasion of privacy and awarding her husband $50,000 for loss of companionship while she recovered. Mr. Kartsotis settled his lawsuit against Justin and his family for an undisclosed amount.

HOW DOES THIS DECISION AFFECT YOU?

The lessons from Justin's case are about location and content. In general, if the school is adversely affected by content you create—no matter where you created it—there will be consequences.

For example, say you're on spring break in Mexico. At an Internet café, you decide to write something offensive or critical of a student or teacher at your school. When school resumes, your comments have spread all over campus and become an issue. Depending on the content and the school's reaction to it, your speech may not be protected.

> **Hate speech** is a criminal law matter that includes the four unprotected speech categories listed on page 31. It is defined as speech intended to degrade or disparage someone or a group based on race, gender, religion, sexual orientation, ethnicity, or other improper classification. Some states use the hate speech designation to enhance penalties for criminal acts. For example, teen Brandon McInerny has been charged with first-degree murder and a hate crime in allegedly shooting his classmate, Larry King, in 2008 (see chapter 8). For more about hate speech and the law, go to the Southern Poverty Law Center at www.splcenter.org.

Is All Speech Protected?

All speech is *not* protected. Four categories of speech do not have the protection of the First Amendment:

1. lewd and obscene speech
2. speech that is profane
3. libelous speech
4. insulting or "fighting words" (those which by their very utterance inflict injury or tend to incite an immediate breach of the peace)

***Purtell v. Mason* (Illinois, 2008)** was a case in which neighbors, Purtell and Mason, engaged in a dispute over Purtell's front yard Halloween display that included tombstones inscribed with criticisms of Mason. The court ruled that since the tombstones were displayed for several weeks without causing a disturbance, the "fighting words" test had not been met, and Mr. Purtell's tombstones constituted protected speech.

***State v. Machado* (California, 1998)** was one of the first cases of its kind, in which 21-year-old Richard J. Machado was prosecuted in 1998 for sending threatening emails. He was an engineering student at the University of California when he was expelled for low grades. He sent emails to dozens of Asian students threatening to "hunt down and kill" them, signing each with "Asian hater." Richard testified that he had been under stress and that the messages were a joke. But the jury heard evidence of a history of bigoted behavior and convicted him. Richard spent a year in jail for his threats, which constituted hate speech.

As you see from Justin's case, and others in this book, unexpected consequences can result from your actions.

The bottom line: Use good judgment when expressing yourself in cyberspace. Your online audience is the world, whether you create content at school or in the privacy of your bedroom.

WHAT IS JUSTIN DOING NOW?

Justin's parents made arrangements for him to finish high school elsewhere. He graduated early and at age 16 entered college. He also finished college early and in 2007 graduated from Duke Law School at age 22. Justin currently practices employment law in Pennsylvania.

> "TODAY, LOOKING BACK, I REALIZE THAT PUBLISHING SUCH A WEB SITE WAS A VERY IMMATURE RESPONSE TO MY FRUSTRATION WITH THE SCHOOL. THOUGH THE WEB SITE WAS A JOKE, THE PUNISHMENT WAS NOT."
> —Justin Swidler

RELATED CASES

Karl Beidler v. North Thurston School District (Washington, 2000)
While a junior at Timberline High School in 1999, Karl Beidler designed a Web page entitled "Lehnis Web." It was a parody of assistant principal Dave Lehnis. It showed him participating in a Nazi book burning, spray painting graffiti on a wall, and drinking beer. Karl was placed on emergency expulsion, because the content of his site was considered appalling and inappropriate. He was transferred to an alternative school for the rest of the year. He returned to Timberline for his senior year without further incident.

Karl fought the school's discipline, but it wasn't until after his graduation that his case was decided. The court stated, "The First Amendment rights of public school students remain constant even in the age of the Internet." Karl was awarded $10,000, plus $52,000 for his lawyers.

Muss v. Beaverton School District (Oregon, 2003)

Carlson Muss was 13 when he created "Carlson's Itch-Bay page" on his home computer and posted it to his AOL account. On the page he poked fun at Canadians, lesbians, classmates, and teachers. He also included off-color jokes and pleas for dates, and listed eight students who "get to live another week," intending it to be taken as a joke. Carlson was reported and evaluated by a psychologist who concluded that he didn't pose a threat to anyone. However, the school expelled him for menacing and disorderly conduct. His application to the district's Art and Communication Magnet Academy was rejected because of his Web site. Carlson sued the school for $100,000, and the court ruled in his favor, reversing his expulsion and settling the case for $20,000. He used part of the settlement for tuition at his new school.

THINGS TO THINK ABOUT

Did you ever think that words alone had so much power? These cases illustrate some of the words that trigger emotions and immediate reactions. Whether you choose words or symbols in your correspondence with others, they may generate an unexpected response regardless of where you communicate them—at home, school, or elsewhere. Words such as "kill" or "bomb," and symbols including a noose or swastika may result in unwanted attention. Do you think there's a difference between writing a note on a piece of paper or posting something online? Why or why not?

Chapter 1: Further Reading and Resources

Brenton, Kyle Wesley. "Bonghits4jesus.com? Tracing the Boundaries of Public School Authority Over Student Cyberspeech." *Minnesota Law Review* 92, no. 4 (2008): 1206–1245.

Eberle, Edward J. "Cross Burning, Hate Speech and Free Speech in America," *Arizona State Law Journal* 36 (Fall 2004): 953–1001.

Gilbert, Melissa L. "'Time-Out' for Student Threats? Imposing a Duty to Protect on School Officials." *UCLA Law Review* 49, no. 3 (February 2002): 917.

CHAPTER 2

How a Careless Email Can Turn Into a Federal Case

Case: *Zachariah Paul v. Franklin Regional School District* (2001)

Act: Creating and distributing an email critical of the school athletic director

Charge: Violating school policy by making offensive remarks about a school official

Bozzuto's Top Ten

10) The school store doesn't sell Twinkies.

9) He is constantly tripping over his own chins.

8) The girls at the 900 numbers keep hanging up on him.

7) For him, becoming Franklin's "Athletic Director" was considered "moving up in the world."

6) He has to use a pencil to type and make phone calls because his fingers are unable to hit only one key at a time.

5) He's just not getting any.

4) He's no longer allowed in any "all you can eat" restaurants.

3) He has constant flashbacks of when he was in high school and the athletes used to pick on him.

2) Because of his extensive gut factor, the man hasn't seen his own penis in over a decade.

1) Even if it weren't for his gut, it would still take a magnifying glass and extensive searching to find it.

Zachariah Paul was a 17-year-old junior at Franklin Regional High School in Pennsylvania. He was on the track team and was upset with the athletic director, Robert Bozzuto, about some of the rules. In 1999, Zach wrote a top ten list at home about Mr. Bozzuto and emailed it to his friends. Another student saw it and made copies that he distributed at school—including in the teacher's lounge.

Zach was called to the principal's office where he admitted to creating the list but denied bringing it to school. This was not Zach's first encounter with the principal. He had written other top ten lists and been warned of discipline if it occurred again. In one list, he described the school librarian as a "book Nazi" and suggested a prank of asking her for books about assembling bombs. The school suspended Zach for 10 days for verbal/written abuse of a staff member, and gave him five Saturday morning detentions. During his suspension he could not participate in any school related activities, including track and field events.

Zach and his mother filed a lawsuit in federal court seeking his immediate reinstatement in school. They claimed that his First Amendment right of free expression had been violated by suspending him for speech that was made off school grounds, in the privacy of his home. Zach was quoted saying, "What I say in my own home is my business." The school argued that Zach was properly suspended for violating school policy by making offensive remarks about a school official. They claimed his top ten list was disruptive, lewd, and obscene.

HOW WOULD YOU DECIDE THIS CASE?

Did Zach go too far in his comments about Mr. Bozzuto? Does it make any difference whether he created the list at home or at school? Should he be punished if another student brought it to school and passed it out? Once you write an email or a blog, are you responsible for its content forever? If not, where does your responsibility end? Should there be consequences for the student who copied the list and distributed it? School policy at Franklin High School allowed suspension for 1 to 10 days for violations of the conduct code. Did Zach's email merit the maximum suspension?

WHAT THE COURT DECIDED

Before Zach's case was heard in federal court, a partial settlement was reached with the school district. Zach wanted to return to school to prepare for his AP exams and finals and to compete with his track team. Zach served 8 of the 10-day suspension, and he was then allowed to return to school. He agreed not to distribute any publications on campus in the future that were critical of the faculty or staff.

Prior to a court hearing regarding a school suspension or expulsion, a student has a *due process* right to be advised of the offense committed, and a right at the hearing to explain his or her side. In Zach's case, he was not provided written notice of the suspension until requested by his mother at the hearing. He had no opportunity to prepare for the hearing. Thus, the court found that his due process rights were violated.

The court also determined that *Tinker*'s "substantial disruption" test (see pages 11–12) applied to Zach's situation. Although Zach's list was written at home and only sent to 20 friends, it was later brought on campus by an unknown person. However, no evidence showed actual disruption at school—teachers were not rendered incapable of teaching or controlling their classes because of the list. In fact, the list was on campus several days before the administration discovered it.

Moreover, according to the court, Zach's speech may have upset Mr. Bozzuto, but it was not threatening. Some may have found it to be rude, abusive, or demeaning. However, disliking or being upset by the content of a student's speech is not an acceptable justification for limiting student expression.

The school argued that they expected some disruption because Mr. Bozzuto had a difficult time doing his job and the school librarian was almost in tears from the "book Nazi" list. The court, however, maintained that these events did not rise to the level of substantial disruption. Regarding the school's claim that Zach's speech was lewd and obscene, the court ruled that since the speech occurred off school grounds, the school was unable to discipline him. Apart from exceptional circumstances, the authority of school officials is limited to the "metes and bounds of the school itself."

The court's decision meant that suspending Zach for the creation of the Bozzuto top ten list violated the First Amendment. The lawsuit was settled with the school district paying Zach and his family $65,000.

How Does This Decision Affect You?

Don't expect any privacy when you send an email—there isn't any. Similar to what happened to Zach, your email may be printed and distributed or forwarded to others. In fact, a glitch in your computer may cause what you write to go out before you even hit "send." As Ian Lake says (in chapter 6), "you can never take it back." Following a two-year court case, Zach won his case against the school, but not until after serving most of the suspension.

> 87% of U.S. teens use email and 93% use the Internet.

Consider the consequences faced by other electronic messengers, both teens and adults:

- In 2007, a 19-year-old in West Virginia intended to send a text to a friend asking him if he wanted to buy some marijuana. However, his friend's number had changed, and the message went to a police officer instead, who arranged to meet with the seller. The teen was arrested and taken to jail.
- In 2008, Connecticut high school principal John Metallo was caught exchanging inappropriate emails with a principal from another

> "WE CANNOT ACCEPT, WITHOUT MORE EVIDENCE, THAT THE CHILDISH AND BOORISH ANTICS OF A MINOR COULD IMPAIR THE ADMINISTRATORS' ABILITIES TO DISCIPLINE STUDENTS AND MAINTAIN CONTROL."
>
> "IF A SCHOOL CAN POINT TO A WELL-FOUNDED EXPECTATION OF DISRUPTION—ESPECIALLY ONE BASED ON PAST INCIDENTS ARISING OUT OF SIMILAR SPEECH—THE RESTRICTION MAY PASS CONSTITUTIONAL MUSTER."
>
> —both quotes from Zachariah Paul's case

school. The two criticized school officials and carried on personal conversations. Metallo quit his job and the second principal was reprimanded.

- Detroit Mayor Kwame Kilpatrick resigned from office after pleading guilty to lying under oath about an affair with his chief of staff. Over 14,000 text messages sent between the two on city-issued cell phones were part of the scandal. In October 2008, Kilpatrick was sentenced to four months in jail and five years probation.

- After a year of steamy emails to "Maria" in Argentina, South Carolina Governor Mark Sanford admitted to the affair. In 2009, he resigned as head of the Republican Governor's Association and put his possible nomination as a 2012 Presidential candidate in jeopardy.

> **Email Safety Tips**
> - Change your password often and don't give it out.
> - Don't open or reply to spam or to harassing or offensive email.
> - Make sure you have an antivirus program running before you open any attachments.
> - Remember: once you put something in writing, it becomes public, whether you want it to or not.

The bottom line: **If you wouldn't say it in person, why say it online? Nothing online is private, not even if you're sharing it with your best friend. Careless or spiteful emails and text messages have been the downfall of many. Don't let it happen to you.**

WHAT IS ZACH DOING NOW?

Zach graduated from high school and went on to college. He joined the Army and served in Afghanistan as a reconnaissance platoon leader.

RELATED CASES

Ryan Kuhl v. Greenwood School District (Arkansas, 2005)

Ryan Kuhl, age 18, and Justin Neal, age 17, were friends at Greenwood High School in Arkansas. They were both seniors and honor students with no history of problems at school. They each created a Web site with links to the other's site. Ryan's site opened with "Fuck Greenwood," criticized the school's orientation as "dreadfully boring," and insulted band members and student athletes. He also included numerous profanities and descriptions of school personnel engaging in sexual acts. Justin's site had an illustration depicting a school assembly where a school official, identified as the assistant principal, is holding a smoking gun next to two students who are apparently shot in the head.

Once the principal became aware of the sites, Ryan and Justin were suspended for three days and ordered to take down their sites. They were told their Web sites were disruptive by creating a "buzz" at school. Both claimed their sites were satire and not intended as threats or to incite anyone to violence. Justin testified that his cartoon represented the "drudgery" of school. The teens sued the school for violating their free speech.

> "SPEECH IS OFTEN PROVOCATIVE AND CHALLENGING. IT MAY INDEED SERVE ITS HIGH PURPOSE WHEN IT INDUCES A CONDITION OF UNREST, CREATES DISSATISFACTION WITH CONDITIONS AS THEY ARE, OR EVEN STIRS PEOPLE TO ANGER."
> —from *Terminiello v. City of Chicago*, 1949

Following a trial in federal court, the court ruled that Ryan's and Justin's postings were protected by the First Amendment and the school had no authority to regulate the content of their Web sites. In the absence of any evidence of actual disruption at school, the court held that "responsible school administrators and teachers must be able to distinguish between true threats and nonthreatening statements couched in less-than-temperate language."

Brandon Beussink v. Woodland School District (Missouri, 1998)
Brandon was a 16-year-old junior at Woodland High School in Missouri. Using a program he found on the Internet, Brandon and his sister worked at home to design and post a Web page that opened with this text:

Brittney & Brandon's Kick Ass Home Page!
Please visit our FUCKED UP High School.
"Home of the fucked up faculty members from HELL!"

Brandon's site made fun of his high school and the administration, teachers, and principal. He created a link to the school's home page and invited readers to email the principal with their opinions. Brandon said he intended only to voice his opinions about school. The principal saw the site and immediately suspended Brandon for 10 days because of the site's content and because it was accessed in a classroom. However, it was another student who showed the page to other students, not Brandon. The principal was also aware that four months earlier Brandon entered an obscenity into the school's screensaver. Brandon returned to school after serving the 10-day suspension. His grades were already low and after missing these additional days, he was failing all of his classes.

Brandon and his mother filed a lawsuit on the basis of free speech. They asked the court to withdraw the suspension and reinstate Brandon's grades before the incident. The court said that discipline for offensive speech must be supported by "more than a mere desire to avoid the discomfort and unpleasantness that always accompany an unpopular viewpoint." The court said further that a core function of free speech is to invite dispute. "It is unpopular speech which needs the protection of the First Amendment which was designed for this very purpose." This incident gave the students at Woodland High the opportunity "to see the protections of the United States Constitution and the Bill of Rights at work."

Brandon won his case, and the school was ordered not to lower his grades based on the suspension or to impose any punishment based on his home page. He was even given permission to repost the page, if he chose to.

Sean O'Brien v. Westlake Board of Education (Ohio, 1998)

Sean O'Brien attended Westlake High School in Ohio. In 1998, he was a 16-year-old junior when he created a Web site that insulted his band teacher with statements such as, "He is an overweight middle-aged man who doesn't like to get haircuts... and favors people who kiss his ass." Sean also included a picture of the teacher and listed his home address and telephone number. Sean was suspended for 10 days and, as a result, received an F in band and lower grades in his other classes.

Sean challenged the discipline in court, which ruled in his favor. The suspension was removed from his record and he returned to school in good standing. The case settled for $30,000, and Sean dropped his lawsuit. In a letter of apology to Sean, the school stated, "the Board recognized that this right to freedom of speech extends to students who, on their own time and with their own resources, engage in speech on the Internet."

Sean's advice for anyone critiquing a teacher or school online is to "Keep it cool. Don't lie."

THINGS TO THINK ABOUT

As you can see from these cases, content is crucial. Regardless of your method of communication (text message, email, Web site, or other means), what you say dictates the outcome in any situation. There are consequences when statements constitute an actual threat. Did you think email and text blunders and embarrassments were limited to kids? Are you surprised by the incidents presented here of adult carelessness and poor judgment? Do you think all the cases were decided fairly? Why or why not? And finally, even though Zach and several others in this chapter "won" their cases in the end, does that mean they "won" from an ethical standpoint? Causing emotional distress to a person or harming a reputation are acts that carry real consequences—no matter what the court rules.

Chapter 2: Further Reading and Resources

Wired Safety • www.wiredsafety.org
Internet education for kids, tweens, and teens and help for victims of cyberbullying. Learn about Teenangels and how you can spread the word about safe and responsible surfing.

Adamovich, Tracy L. "Return to Sender: Off-Campus Student Speech Brought On-Campus by Another Student." *St. John's Law Review* 82, no. 3 (Summer 2008): 1087–1113.

Calvert, Clay, and Robert D. Richards. "Free Speech and the Right to Offend: Old Wars, New Battles, Different Media." *Georgia State University Law Review* 18, no. 3 (Spring 2002): 671–695.

Freeman, Simone Marie. "Upholding Students' Due Process Rights: Why Students Are in Need of Better Representation at, and Alternatives to, School Suspension Hearings." *Family Court Review* 45, no. 4 (October 2007): 638–656.

Tuneski, Alexander G. "Online, Not on Grounds: Protecting Student Internet Speech." *Virginia Law Review* 89, no. 1 (2003): 139.

CHAPTER 3

Balancing Student Rights and School Responsibilities

Case: *Justin Layshock v. Hermitage School District* (2007)

Act: creating an unflattering fake MySpace profile for his school principal

Charge: being disrespectful, causing disruption, using profane language, and using a school photo without permission

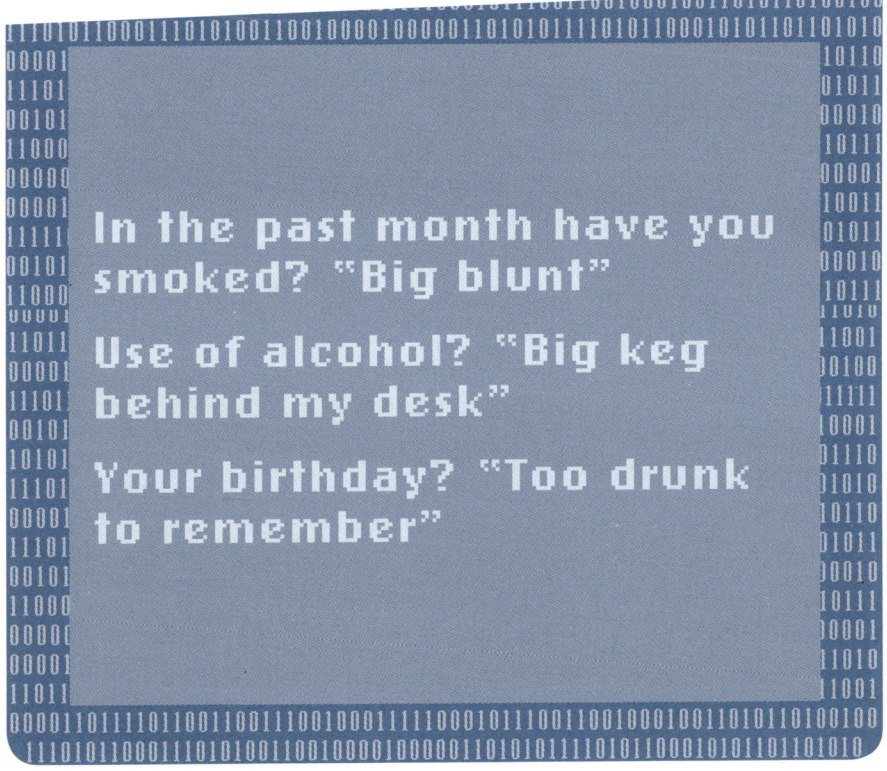

In the past month have you smoked? "Big blunt"

Use of alcohol? "Big keg behind my desk"

Your birthday? "Too drunk to remember"

The previous is part of the fake MySpace profile of Eric Trosch, principal of Hickory High School in Pennsylvania. Justin Layshock created the profile in 2005 on his grandmother's computer. He added a picture of Mr. Trosch taken from the school's Web site, and referred to Mr. Trosch as a "big steroid freak," a "big whore," and "a big hard ass."

Justin was a 17-year-old senior with a 3.3 GPA who took advanced placement classes. He was college bound and had already applied to four universities. He also tutored middle school students. He told a few friends about his MySpace profile for Mr. Trosch, and word spread quickly to most of the student body. Justin attempted to delete the page and apologized to the principal. The school contacted MySpace.com and the profile was officially removed from the site.

Justin and his father were called to the police station for an interview, but no criminal charges were filed. Several weeks later, the school met with Justin and his mother. The school decided to discipline Justin for being disrespectful, causing disruption, using profane language, and using a school photo without permission. He received a 10-day out-of-school suspension. When he returned, he was placed in an alternative program and banned from any extra activities for the rest of the school year. That included his AP classes and graduation ceremony.

Justin and his parents went to court and asked for immediate relief. The alternative program was designed for students with behavior and attendance problems. They only met for three hours a day and Justin didn't receive any of the assignments from his regular classes. His parents further argued that the school overstepped their constitutional bounds by disciplining Justin for his off-campus activity, when, as parents, they were responsible for raising him.

Justin explained that the MySpace page he created was a nonthreatening, nonobscene parody of his principal. As such, he argued that the First Amendment protected his speech. The school responded that considerable disruption occurred at school when so many students accessed the site that the school had to shut down its computer system. Several classes that relied on the computers had to be canceled, and the school's technology support person had to install additional firewall protections.

HOW WOULD YOU DECIDE THIS CASE?

Although it may not be nice or polite, is it wrong— or even illegal—to poke fun at someone? Should there be limits on who you can target? For example, should school principals or teachers be off-limits? If yes, where do you draw the line? Who else is off-limits? Who isn't? Is that fair? Do you agree with *Tinker*'s "substantial disruption test" that many courts use in these cases (see pages 11–12)? Do you think the test should be limited or broadened? Should Justin's senior status and academic standing be a factor in determining his punishment?

WHAT THE COURT DECIDED

The court encouraged Justin and the school to reach a settlement on the issues. The school modified the punishment by allowing Justin to return to his regular classes, participate in after-school activities, and attend his graduation. Justin's First Amendment claim remained to be decided. The court was faced with balancing a student's freedom of expression with the school's right and responsibility to maintain an environment conducive to learning. The court made the following comments concerning the Internet:

"The mere fact that the Internet may be accessed at school does not authorize school officials to become censors of the world-wide web. Public schools are vital institutions, but their reach is not unlimited. Schools have an undoubted right to control conduct within the scope of their activities, but they must share the supervision of children with other, equally vital, institutions such as families, churches, community organizations, and the judicial system."

The court considered the tests presented by both *Tinker* and *Fraser* (see pages 12–13) in weighing Justin's argument that his parody was protected speech. The questions at the heart of the matter are: Was the school disrupted? Did Justin's language constitute obscene or lewd speech?

The court's answer to both questions was no. The evidence connecting the parody to any disturbance at school was insufficient. Regarding obscene speech, the court said, "While the profile is certainly juvenile and lacks serious value," it does not rise to the level of obscenity. The court also dismissed the parents' claim that their right to discipline Justin was affected in any way. In fact, Justin was grounded by his parents. The school district's appeal remains pending at the time of this book's publication.

HOW DOES THIS DECISION AFFECT YOU?

The decision in Justin's case is one of the latest in a 10-year history of courts wrestling to balance student rights with the responsibilities of schools. A fine line exists between protected and unprotected speech. Schools and courts often disagree over what is acceptable speech and how best to allow schools to operate without judicial interference.

The time will come when one of these cases will be argued before the U.S. Supreme Court, which will determine how far a student can go with Internet expression and how far a school can reach beyond its boundaries in disciplining students. Until then, however, school districts must recognize that the First Amendment applies to students. Likewise, students need to understand the school's role in providing a safe and appropriate educational environment.

> "STUDENTS USING SOCIAL NETWORKING SITES ARE IN MANY WAYS PRACTICING THE KINDS OF 21ST CENTURY SKILLS WE WANT THEM TO DEVELOP TO BE SUCCESSFUL TODAY."
> —Professor Christine Greenhow, University of Minnesota
>
> "WRITING FOR AN AUDIENCE MOTIVATES TEENS TO WRITE AND WRITE WELL. DISCUSSION BOARDS, BLOGS, AND WIKIS GIVE STUDENTS A REAL AUDIENCE, RATHER THAN THE OUTDATED 'STUDENT-TO-TEACHER' WRITING OF THE PAST."
> —PEW Internet and American Life Project, 2008

The bottom line: The U.S. Constitution guarantees protection of individual rights. This applies to students as well as teachers. However, depending on the intent and content, your speech may not always be protected as one of your individual rights.

WHAT IS JUSTIN DOING NOW?

After Justin won his initial court case in 2007, Principal Trosch filed a lawsuit against him, claiming damage to his reputation, humiliation, and impaired earning capacity. The federal court determined that Justin's statements were not made with actual malice and that Mr. Trosch could not recover punitive damages.

Justin graduated and is now attending college.

RELATED CASES

Draker v. Schreiber (Texas, 2008)

In 2006, high school student Benjamin Schreiber created a fake MySpace profile for his vice principal, Anna Draker, at Clark High School in Texas. The site included her name, photo, and several false statements about her sexual preferences and activities. Benjamin portrayed Ms. Draker as a lesbian, which she was not, and added lewd comments, pictures, and graphics. Ms. Draker was married with small children and was devastated by what she saw on the Web site.

Ms. Draker sued Benjamin and his parents for defamation, negligence, and intentional infliction of emotional distress. She claimed that his parents failed to properly supervise his use of the Internet. The trial court dismissed her lawsuit because

Students Rate Their Teachers

In 2009, a teacher in Germany lost her case against students who gave her a "D" as a teacher. A Web site allowed students to anonymously grade their teachers. The court recognized the right of students to exchange ideas.

A Principal Defends Her Students

Alaska high school principal Cyd Duffin filed a lawsuit for defamation and invasion of privacy against MySpace in March 2009. Someone had created a fake profile in her name depicting her as a racist drug-user with a sexually transmitted disease. The page also attacked hearing-impaired students and the racial composition of the school.

Mrs. Duffin was more upset about the attacks against her students than those against her. She stated, "Go ahead and hit me, but don't hit my kids." MySpace was dismissed from the case after they disclosed the names of those who created the fake page. Two students confessed and were disciplined.

the "exaggerated and derogatory statements" Benjamin made on MySpace were not defamatory as a matter of law, and because no facts could be objectively verified. Furthermore, Ms. Draker failed to specify any independent facts to support her claim of emotional distress.

Benjamin admitted to creating the Web page and was suspended for three days. He was also charged with retaliation and fraudulent use of identifying information. He was placed on probation and required to perform community service and participate in counseling.

State of Texas v. Solis (Texas, 2006)

In 2006, a 14-year-old girl in Texas met 19-year-old Pete Solis on MySpace. The girl allegedly lied about her age online and Pete thought she was 18. To gain her trust, he claimed to be a high school senior and a member of the football team. She gave him her cell phone number and when they met in person, he sexually assaulted her. Solis pleaded guilty to injury to a child and was sentenced to 90 days in jail. The girl and her mother sued MySpace for $30 million for not preventing sexual predators from contacting minors on their Web site. The lawsuit was dismissed, with the court ruling that the duty to protect children belongs to parents, not to MySpace.

Social Networking Stats

- In a 2008 study, 75% of the students with a personal profile on a social networking site report using it for creativity, communication skills, and being open to new and diverse views.

- 74% of parents know whether their kids have a social networking profile. 65% of parents report checking what Web sites their kids viewed after they get offline.

- MySpace had roughly 125 million active users worldwide in December 2008, resulting in 43 billion page views that month. Users must be at least 14 years old and are encouraged to block any member considered a threat and contact the police. MySpace reserves the right to terminate any user for posting threats or behaving inappropriately, which includes creating fake profiles. You can also ask MySpace to remove offensive material, which they often do.

THINGS TO THINK ABOUT

If an online relationship formed through a social networking site results in actual harm to a user, do you think the site should take some responsibility? What do you think about students who single out a particular teacher, administrator, or coach to target on a site like Facebook or MySpace? Is it an attempt at humor, or is it done out of frustration or anger? It's certainly easier today to criticize someone in cyberspace than in person, but is it worth it, even if your speech is protected and you win your case? Why or why not? Would you comment on a teacher's hygiene, physical appearance, or sex life to his or her face? Why do it online? Besides the teacher, who else might be affected by your comments? In what ways?

- Facebook claimed roughly 222 million active users internationally in December 2008, totaling 80 billion monthly page views. It has similar anti-bullying policies as MySpace, but has a minimum member age of 13.
- In 2008, Facebook and MySpace reached an agreement with 49 states to institute changes to protect young users from online predators and inappropriate material. Users under 18 are required to confirm that they have read the Web site's safety tips. A "Report Abuse" icon can be found on their sites and inappropriate material will be removed within 24 hours.

Social Networking Safety Tips

- Don't say you're older than you are in order to become a member of a site. Age requirements are in place for your protection.
- Don't post anything that could embarrass you later or expose you to danger.
- Protect your privacy. Set your profile to private.
- Don't display personal information on your profile such as your home address and phone number.
- Report harassment, hate speech, and inappropriate content.
- Don't get caught by a phishing scam—keep your username and password private.
- Avoid in-person meetings. If you do choose to meet someone you met online, be sure to meet during the day in a public place, bring someone with you, and tell an adult your plans beforehand.

Chapter 3: Further Reading and Resources

Dayton, John, and Anne Proffitt Dupre. "Morse Code: How School Speech Takes a ('Bong') Hit," *West's Education Law Reporter* 233 (August 2008): 503.

Hudson, David L. Jr. "Student Online Expression: What Do the Internet and MySpace Mean for Students' First Amendment Rights?" First Amendment Center. Available at Georgetown Law Library's Digital Archive Collection. cdm16064.contentdm.oclc.org/cdm/ref/collection/p266901coll4/id/3468 (accessed April 11, 2014).

CHAPTER 4

Political Expression or Intentional Harassment?

Case: *A.B. v. State of Indiana* (2008)

Act: posting comments on two Web sites criticizing a principal and school policy

Charge: harassment and obscenity

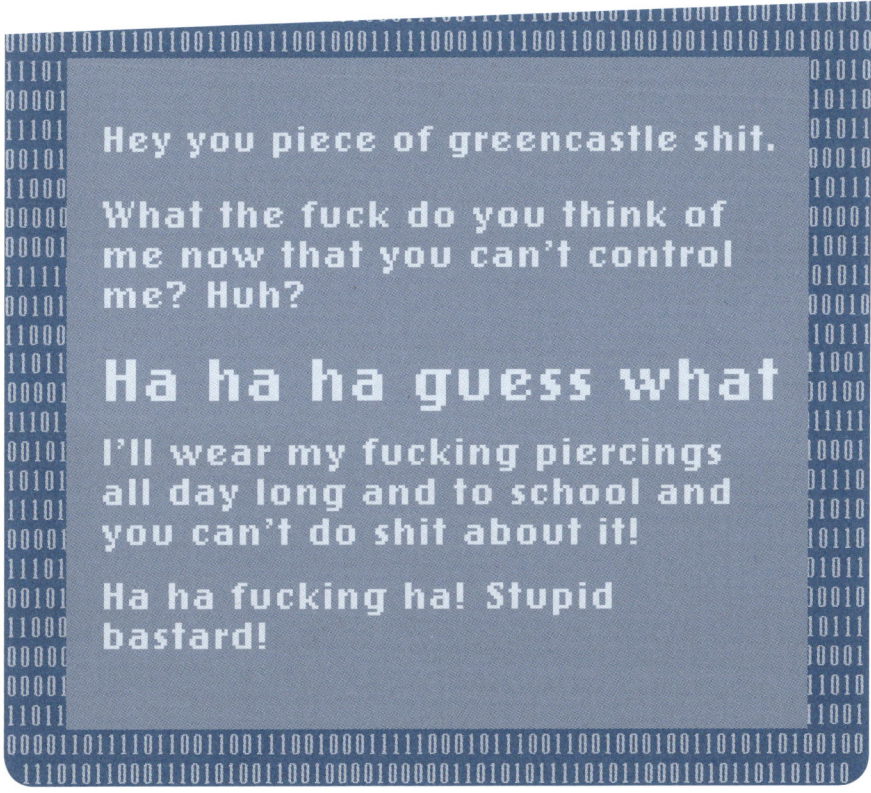

Hey you piece of greencastle shit.

What the fuck do you think of me now that you can't control me? Huh?

Ha ha ha guess what

I'll wear my fucking piercings all day long and to school and you can't do shit about it!

Ha ha fucking ha! Stupid bastard!

A.B. was a 14-year-old middle school student at Greencastle Middle School, which had a policy against wearing body piercings at school. A.B. opposed the policy and later, while attending a different school, decided to express her feelings about it online.

In 2006, Shawn Gobert was the principal of Greencastle. Mr. Gobert learned that a derogatory Web page about the administration had been created on MySpace. A.B.'s friend had created a "Gobert" page and invited her to take a look. A.B. posted her own comments on the site, including "die . . . gobert . . . die." Then A.B. created her own MySpace page under the name "Fuck Mr. Gobert and Greencastle Schools." She posted a total of six messages on the two different sites, including the message shown on page 53.

> When kids get in trouble with the law, the courts protect their identity by using only their initials such as **T.J.**, or first name and last initial, like **Tom J.** Courts respect the privacy of minors, but not at the expense of victims or justice.

Two weeks later, the state of Indiana filed a delinquency petition against A.B. in juvenile court, charging her with eight counts of harassment. The court dismissed two of the counts and found A.B. guilty of the remaining six. She was placed on probation for nine months. A.B. appealed the juvenile court's decision that her postings were obscene and therefore not protected by the First Amendment as political speech. Her case went to the Indiana Court of Appeals.

HOW WOULD YOU DECIDE THIS CASE?

Admittedly, A.B.'s tirade against the school was strong and contained offensive language. But do words alone forfeit your right to speak? Did A.B. harm or injure anyone? Was her criticism of the school's piercing policy a crime, or was it a legitimate expression of her point of view?

Does it make any difference that A.B. was not attending Greencastle at the time of the incident?

If the appeals court maintains the harassment conviction, what lesson do you see here for students wishing to speak up on school issues? If the conviction is overturned, what does that say to school officials attempting to create a safe learning environment for all students?

WHAT THE COURT DECIDED

The Indiana Court of Appeals did not address the issue of obscenity, but ruled instead on the basis of protected political speech. A.B. was upset with the school's dress code and vented her displeasure in writing. The court held that, "While we have little regard for A.B.'s use of vulgar epithets, we conclude that her overall message constitutes political speech."

The court was mindful that political expression is not shielded from all criminal liability. If your expression causes harm to another, then it may be a crime. In this case, however, no evidence showed that A.B.'s postings inflicted personal harm or injury on anyone. Her conviction for harassment violated her right to speak and was therefore dismissed. The prosecutor took the case one step further and appealed to the Indiana Supreme Court.

The state supreme court agreed that A.B.'s conviction was wrong, but for a different reason. They decided the harassment charges filed against A.B. had not been proven. Under Indiana law, harassment includes the intent to harass, annoy, or alarm another person. This means that A.B., in posting her comments, must have intended Mr. Gobert to read them. However, what she wrote on her friend's private profile page was not viewable by the general public, only by accepted friends. Therefore the court ruled that A.B. had no "expectation that her conduct would likely come to the attention of Mr. Gobert."

A.B. won her case before two appellate courts, each for different reasons: protected speech and no intent to harass.

HOW DOES THIS DECISION AFFECT YOU?

The criminal laws of each state provide notice of what behavior is unacceptable. Any charge filed against a person must be proven beyond a reasonable doubt. In A.B.'s case, the state failed to prove that she intended to harass the principal. If the state had proven intent, then her speech may not have been protected. The facts of every case must be carefully reviewed before consequences are imposed.

This decision also supports the concept of privacy in personal postings on sites that are not accessible to the public. That's not to say that someone couldn't send your comments out to the world from a private page. But since Mr. Gobert didn't have access to A.B.'s comments made on a private page, he didn't know everything she said.

> "IT IS CLEAR THAT SCHOOL AUTHORITIES ARE STATE ACTORS FOR PURPOSES OF FREEDOM OF EXPRESSION AND ARE SUBJECT TO THE COMMANDS OF THE FIRST AMENDMENT."
> —from A.B.'s decision at the Indiana Court of Appeals

> "WE ALSO OBSERVE THAT IT IS EVEN MORE PLAUSIBLE THAT A.B. MERELY INTENDED TO AMUSE AND GAIN APPROVAL OR NOTORIETY FROM HER FRIENDS, AND/OR TO GENERALLY VENT ANGER FOR HER PERSONAL GRIEVANCES."
> —from A.B.'s decision at the Indiana Supreme Court

The bottom line: Courts may disagree and come to different conclusions when reviewing a case. A.B. could have lost just as easily if her case had been heard before another court, as you'll see from other cases in this book.

WHAT IS A.B. DOING NOW?

A.B. has chosen to remain anonymous, which is her right. All attempts to contact her have been unsuccessful.

Do You Know Who's Reading Your Profile?

School resource officers and campus police are known to scan Facebook and MySpace pages to monitor crime at school, break up fights, and check gang activity. Runaways who stay in touch with friends online have been located and helped by law enforcement. Teen discussions online about drugs, sex, and violence may be public information and therefore viewable by the police.

Dr. Megan Moreno at the University of Washingon recently conducted a study of teen MySpace users. She found that more than half of 18-year-old users mentioned sex, violence, or substance use on their profiles. Following a brief email from Dr. Moreno warning that such posts could come back to haunt them, 42% of users changed their profiles. The email read in part: "I noticed something on your MySpace profile that concerned me. You seemed to be quite open about sexual issues or other behaviors such as drinking or smoking. Are you sure that's a good idea? After all, if I could see it, anybody could."

> After his office scanned local students' online public profiles, a Virginia county sheriff commented that, "It's crazy, the things they put on there. They seem to think they're invisible."

RELATED CASES

State v. McEvoy and Gagnon (Colorado, 2007)

"My fists are my best friends—you're about to meet them too." This was one of several threatening lyrics in a rap song posted online by 18-year-old Jonathan McEvoy and 19-year-old Nicholas Gagnon. The song was written to retaliate against a group of students at Loveland High School in Colorado. The boys were suspended for a week and the song was removed from the Web. They were charged with criminal harassment, but since the words were not specifically directed toward anyone, the charges were eventually dropped.

Dan Sullivan v. Houston Independent School District (Texas, 1973)

This is an early case involving suppression of student speech. Although not involving the Internet, it laid the foundation for future decisions about student expression. Dan Sullivan wrote *Pflashlyte*, an underground newspaper critical of his high school and the administration. He sold the paper across the street from the school, but copies found their way onto campus. Dan was expelled for not following "prior submission" rules set by his school, which the court said were reasonable. Students could distribute their writings on campus before and after school, but only after being reviewed by the principal. Dan had repeatedly violated the policy and the expulsion was upheld.

Thomas v. Granville Central School District (New York, 1979)

In another early case involving student free speech, Donna Thomas and three friends, all seniors at Granville High School, wrote the newspaper *Hard Times* and sold it off campus. It contained some sexual content and was self-described as "uncensored, vulgar, and immoral." However, it failed to disrupt any school activities. Once the paper came to the school's attention, the seniors were suspended for five days. The students took the matter to court. Ruling in the students' favor, the court stated, "The risk is simply too great that school officials will punish protected speech and thereby inhibit future expression."

Caught Online

Mandi Jackson's cheerleading coach at Pearl High School in Mississippi required all of the girls to give her their passwords to their social networking accounts. The girls believed it was so the coaches could check their profiles for photos of drinking or smoking. Fourteen-year-old Mandi considered her coach an authority figure and offered up her password. The coach found profanity-laced messages Mandi had written to another girl, and she shared them with teachers, the principal, and the school superintendant. Mandi was removed from cheerleading and was shunned by other students. She and her parents sued the school district and coach in July 2009 for $100 million, claiming an invasion of privacy and a violation of free speech and due process. The lawsuit

THINGS TO THINK ABOUT

We all have moments of anger or frustration. It's human nature to react when life presents us with a challenge or obstacle. But it's *how* you react that may change your life. What could A.B have done differently to express herself and avoid the problems she created? Even though she won her case in court, the outcome in her case or in any of these cases could have gone the other way, especially if the victim suffered physical or mental injury. Try putting yourself in the shoes of the victims in these cases. What, if any, difference does it make in how you view them?

remains pending at the time of this book's publication.

In 2008, 13 Eden Prairie High School students in Minnesota were seen partying in pictures on Facebook. The pictures came to the attention of the school and the students were suspended from their sports teams for violating the school's code of conduct. The school explained that it was not prowling social networking sites looking for violations, but could not ignore student photos brought to its attention.

Tips for Smart Social Networking

Before you apply for a job or college, do a Google search of your name. If there are any embarrassing photos or other materials, ask to have them removed before someone making a decision about your life sees them. Here are results from a 2008 survey of over 300 top U.S. colleges:

- 10% of admissions officers acknowledged looking at social networking sites to evaluate applicants.
- 38% said that what they saw negatively affected their views of the applicant.
- Potential deal breakers included bad language and photos or videos of illegal activities or inappropriate behavior.

After removing any questionable material, go on the offensive. Fill your Facebook, MySpace, or other personal sites with all the great things you're doing. If you volunteer, blog about it. Replace sexy pictures with travel photos. Make it so the first information that comes up about you in a Google search is a great reflection of yourself.

Chapter 4: Further Reading and Resources

Netsmartz Workshop • www.netsmartz.org/Teens
NetSmartz Workshop is a program of the National Center for Missing & Exploited Children, which offers free Internet safety resources. Find out how to stay in control of your online profile, and watch videos of real-life stories told by teens who have been victims of Internet exploitation.

Decker, Charlotte. "Cyber Crime 2.0: An Argument to Update the United States Criminal Code to Reflect the Changing Nature of Cyber Crime." *Southern California Law Review* 81, no. 5 (July 2008): 959–1016.

Simpson, Scott R. "Report Card: Grading the Country's Response to Columbine." *Buffalo Law Review* 53, no. 1 (Winter 2005): 415–458.

Williams, Kara D. "Public Schools vs. MySpace and Facebook: The Newest Challenge to Student Speech Rights." *University of Cincinnati Law Review* 76, no. 2 (Winter 2008): 707–732.

CHAPTER 5

When Does School Discipline Become Unconstitutional?

Case: *Avery Doninger v. Lewis Mills High School* (2008)

Act: making critical remarks about school officials in her personal blog

Charge: using vulgar language, showing disrespect, causing disruption at school, engaging in behavior inappropriate for a school officer

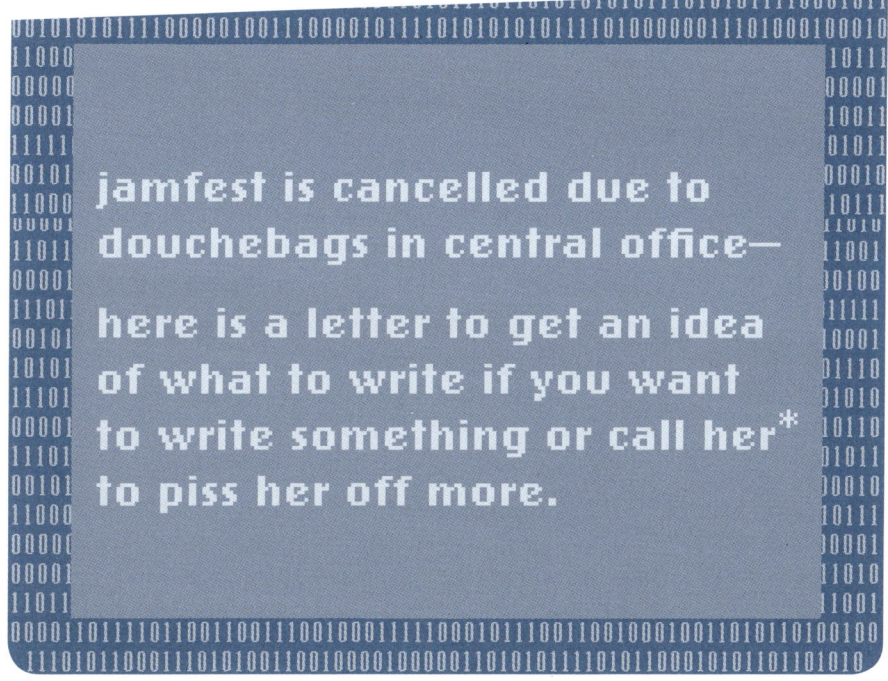

jamfest is cancelled due to douchebags in central office—

here is a letter to get an idea of what to write if you want to write something or call her* to piss her off more.

* referring to the school superintendent

In 2007, Avery was a 16-year-old junior at Lewis Mills High School in Connecticut. She was the class secretary and, as a member of the student council, she helped plan the school's annual "Jamfest." This was a battle-of-the-bands concert held at the end of the school year. It had already been canceled three times and faced another rescheduling because the school's sound technician wasn't available.

Opposing this latest development, the student council decided to ask the community to persuade school officials to let Jamfest take place as scheduled. The four council members, including Avery, went to the computer lab and sent an email asking recipients to contact the school. This resulted in numerous calls and emails to the principal and superintendent.

After sending the email from school, Avery went home and wrote the message on page 61 on her LiveJournal blog. She later explained that the purpose of posting her entry was "to encourage more people to contact the administration" about Jamfest. The matter was settled and the concert was successfully held at the school. The school maintained that Jamfest was never canceled.

When the principal became aware of Avery's blog, she decided the message was inappropriate for a class officer. It failed to display civility and was not the way to resolve issues with the school. Avery had previously been advised by the principal about how to handle disputes with the school. Thus, she wrote a letter of apology to the school superintendent for the "tone and language" of her blog. As punishment, Avery was not allowed to run for senior class secretary. The school also prohibited any student from wearing "Team Avery" T-shirts to school. However, although not on the ballot, she won the election as a write-in candidate. The school did not allow her to take office, and the second place winner became class secretary. There was no disciplinary action noted in Avery's school record.

Avery and her mother filed a lawsuit in the Connecticut state court asking for a new election in which she could campaign, and for damages due to emotional distress. The school stood by its decision asserting vulgar language, disrespect, and possible disruption at school. Although three other students signed the initial email, only Avery was disciplined due to her LiveJournal blog. Since the case raised free speech issues, it was transferred to federal court, which has jurisdiction to rule on First Amendment challenges.

HOW WOULD YOU DECIDE THIS CASE?

Avery was quoted saying, "This case isn't just about me wanting to become my class secretary. There is a bigger issue involved and that is student speech rights. You have to stand up for the little things that make democracy really work in the big world."

Are you offended by Avery's use of the word "douchebag" in her blog? *Webster's Dictionary* defines *douche bag* as "an unattractive or offensive person." She was referring to people in the central office. What could Avery have done differently to accomplish her goal of building community support for the concert? Was calling for a telephone and email barrage on the administration the best way to make her point? Did the school overreact? Did the punishment fit the crime, considering Avery was a class officer? Based on the other cases you've read in this book so far, are you surprised by the school's action? Why or why not?

WHAT THE COURT DECIDED

The federal court held that Avery, as a student leader, had a particular responsibility to demonstrate qualities of good citizenship at all times—on and off campus. Her blog was viewed as offensive and, although it was written at home, it was considered on-campus speech because it promoted outside influence on a school matter. Avery's choice of words and attempt to irritate the superintendent violated school policy.

The court recognized that its role was limited in determining whether the school authorities' punishment was constitutionally acceptable. "The court defers to their experience and judgment, and has no wish to insert itself into the intricacies of a school's decision-making process." Avery was not barred from running for office because of the color of her skin, her religion, or her politics. She was prevented from campaigning because of the language in her blog and the risk of substantial disruption at school that it created.

The court said Avery was free to express her opinions about the administration in any manner she liked. Yet she did not have a First Amendment right to run for a voluntary extracurricular position as a student leader while engaging in uncivil and offensive communications regarding school officials. "Her chosen words, that others should call the 'douchebags' in the central office to 'piss them off more' were hardly conducive to cooperative conflict resolution" expected from a school leader. Avery's request for a new election was denied.

In January 2009, the federal court rejected Avery's claim of intentional infliction of emotional distress. "If courts and legal scholars cannot discern the contours of First Amendment protections for student Internet speech, then it is certainly unreasonable to expect school administrators . . . to predict where the line between on- and off-campus speech will be drawn in this new digital era." However, in May 2009, the case was returned to the appellate court to reconsider Avery's First Amendment free speech claim regarding her blog and whether the school violated her rights in banning the "Team Avery" shirts at school. Her appeal remains pending at the time of this book's publication.

In an interesting turn of events, Avery's principal was disciplined in 2008 for violating Avery's privacy. Responding to an email criticizing her handling of Avery's case, Principal Niehoff disclosed private information about Avery. Ms. Niehoff was suspended for two days without pay and ordered to attend a workshop on federal student privacy laws.

> **What Is Student Privacy?**
> In 1974, Congress passed the Family Educational Rights and Privacy Act. The law grants students certain rights including the right to inspect and review their educational records, request an amendment to inaccurate or misleading entries, request a hearing, consent to disclosure, and file a complaint with the U.S. Department of Education if their rights are violated. At age 18, all rights under the Act transfer to the student. The school may disclose some directory information without consent such as name, date of birth, and dates of attendance. However, enrollment records, grades, class schedules, disciplinary records, and transcripts are confidential. A student may make a formal request to limit disclosure of directory information.

How Does This Decision Affect You?

The court determined that it was the content of her blog that disqualified Avery from class office. Her choice of words and call for disruption crossed the line, especially for a class officer. The court hinted in its ruling that Avery's case was a close call. "Educators will inevitably make mistakes in carrying out this delicate responsibility" regarding the right of dissent and proper respect for authority. Unless clearly unconstitutional, however, courts hesitate to intervene in school disciplinary matters.

> *The bottom line:* If you hold a position of responsibility, always consider your words and actions—whether in school or out. If deemed inappropriate, they may put your position and your reputation in jeopardy.

> "THIS WAS A 16-YEAR-OLD GIRL TRYING TO FIND HER POLITICAL VOICE, AND SHE DID IT CLUMSILY. HIGH SCHOOL SHOULD BE A TRAINING GROUND FOR CITIZENSHIP, AND IF WE SQUASH STUDENTS' CLUMSY ATTEMPTS AT POLITICAL ACTIVISM, IT IS A VERY DANGEROUS THING."
> —Lauren Doninger, Avery's mother

What Is Avery Doing Now?

Avery graduated from high school in 2008. She spent a year in AmeriCorps before going to college.

In comments about her case, Avery said, "It would have been so much easier for me to say 'Oh well' and move on like so many people do. However, if we can't stand up for our civil liberties in our own communities, how are we ever supposed to uphold democracy nationally or internationally? If we don't protect our rights, they will slowly erode. We are the future leaders and we have to be willing to question authority, be willing to tell the truth, and not cower for fear of consequences."

Avery Doninger

RELATED CASES

Garrido v. Krasnasky (Vermont, 2008)
In 2008, a Vermont court ruled that freedom of expression includes the right to freely comment on a blog. In this particular case, a husband made sexual references and occasional profanities in his blog about his wife and their pending divorce. He also posted pages that he scanned from her diary. The court warned the husband that his freedom of expression did not protect him from legal action by the wife for stealing her property (the diary) or from harassment claims.

The World's Oldest Blogger

Calling herself "the world's oldest blogger," 97-year-old Maria Amelia Lopez wrote about everything from life in Spain under a dictatorship to the U.S.-led invasion of Iraq. Her blog attracted more than 1.7 million hits since she started blogging at age 95. Ms. Lopez passed away in 2009, but her words live on at amis95.blogspot.com. She encouraged elder people to get wired, stating, "I did not know there was so much goodness in the world."

The Benefits of Blogging & Texting

Blogs, social networking sites, email, IM, and texting all have potential for improving a student's ability to write.

> 30% of online teens write blogs and 54% read blogs.

"Students are savvy and will learn to adjust the way they write to fit the audience," says Professor Richard Sterling at the Graduate School of Education at Berkeley University.

The informality of email, blogging, and texting is seeping into schoolwork. A 2008 study indicated that proper punctuation and capitalization is being left out, while text shortcuts like LOL (laugh out loud) and emoticons are appearing. However, text-message abbreviations and simplifications have been shown *not* to be detrimental to students' spelling.

What are some specific benefits of digital writing?

It increases your typing speed. Morgan Pozgar of Pennsylvania, age 13, was crowned the first LG U.S. National Texting Champion in 2007. She was one of 300 competitors in New York City who were tested for speed and accuracy in typing. She won by typing a 151-character phrase without any typos or

Quon v. Arch Wireless Operating Co. (California, 2008)

A federal court ruled in 2008 that an expectation of privacy at work on your cell phone exists regarding text messages. Your boss may not be allowed to read your messages unless you agree or you used the company's servers. Text messages are normally managed by outside providers, thus limiting an employer's reach.

In the Matter of Texting at Monarch High (Colorado, 2007)

In 2007, a security officer at Monarch High School in Colorado saw a 16-year-old sophomore smoking in the school parking lot. He took the student to the

abbreviations in 42 seconds. Her prize? $25,000 and bragging rights. The contest's sponsor, LG, upped the first prize to $50,000 in 2008, and the winner was 20-year-old Nathan Schwartz of Ohio. Kate Moore, age 15, of Iowa took first place in 2009.

It could get you money for college. If you like to blog and plan on going to college, take a look at www.collegenet.com. The site invites students to write on topics ranging from breaking news events to local and national politics or college life. Weekly tuition awards up to $5,000 are given to the student receiving the most votes for his or her blog.

It could help with your career. A Dutch company hires computer-savvy 15- and 16-year-olds to tutor technology-challenged bankers, lawyers, and other professionals. The teens present a workshop covering text messaging, photo sharing, and voice mail. They are paid $15 per hour and have a chance to make future business contacts.

> "THE LOSS OF FIRST AMENDMENT FREEDOMS FOR EVEN MINIMAL PERIODS OF TIME NORMALLY CONSTITUTES IRREPARABLE INJURY. SCHOOLTEACHERS AND OFFICIALS MUST TEACH OUR CHILDREN TO THINK CRITICALLY AND TO OBJECT TO WHAT THEY PERCEIVE AS INJUSTICE. BUT SCHOOL OFFICIALS MUST ALSO INCULCATE THE VALUES OF CIVIL DISCOURSE AND RESPECT FOR THE DIGNITY OF EVERY PERSON. THAT IS AN ESPECIALLY DIFFICULT BALANCE TO ACHIEVE IN A SOCIETY WHERE THE PUBLIC DISCOURSE TO WHICH STUDENTS ARE EXPOSED IS OFTEN CRUDE AND EVEN HURTFUL."
>
> —from Avery Doninger's court decisions, 2007–2008

Tip: Don't write anything online you wouldn't want posted on a bulletin board at school. Remember, www also means "the **w**hole **w**orld is **w**atching."

> "FAILURE TO HARNESS THE POTENTIAL ENERGY OF STUDENT BLOGGERS AND DIGITAL WRITERS WOULD PROVE A TERRIBLE MISSTEP AT THIS JUNCTION IN AMERICAN EDUCATION. WE CAN SCORN YOUTH FOR THEIR EMOTICONS, CONDEMN THEIR ABBREVIATIONS, AND LAMENT THE TIME STUDENTS SPEND WRITING IN WAYS ADULTS DO NOT UNDERSTAND. OR, WE CAN EMBRACE THE WRITING THAT STUDENTS DO EVERY DAY, HELP THEM LEARN TO USE THEIR SOCIAL NETWORKING TOOLS TO CREATE LEARNING NETWORKS, AND ULTIMATELY SHOW THEM HOW THE BEST ELEMENTS OF THEIR INFORMAL COMMUNICATION CAN LEAD THEM TO SUCCESS IN THEIR FORMAL WRITING."
> —Justin Reich, Harvard Graduate School of Education

office where his cell phone was taken, read, and some of the text messages were transcribed. Other students also had their cell phones confiscated and messages transcribed.

The students and their parents claimed in court that, without any suspicion of criminal activity, their right to privacy was violated. An agreement was reached in 2008 when the school district agreed to limit searches of students' cell phones. Before reading any cell phone messages, the school official must get permission from the student or parent, unless there is an imminent threat to public safety.

THINGS TO THINK ABOUT

Have you heard the expression "justice is blind"? Or noticed that Lady Justice is portrayed in pictures or on court buildings blindfolded and holding a set of scales? Enforcing laws is an exercise in balancing the rights of individuals, regardless of their race, sex, class, or other demographic. Avery Doninger's principal disciplined Avery for her actions, and later, the principal was likewise reprimanded for violating Avery's rights. Ideally, the law is administered even-handedly—no one has the upper hand, regardless of age or station in life. Do you agree with this? Why or why not?

The Most Valued Right

Generations ago, the United States Supreme Court commented on an individual's right to privacy. It referred to your "right to be let alone—the most comprehensive of rights and the right most valued by civilized men."
—*Olmstead v. United States* (1928)

Chapter 5: Further Reading and Research

Electronic Frontier Foundation • www.eff.org
Want to know how to protect your civil liberties in the digital world? Explore this up-to-date, information-packed site to learn about the law and your online rights.

Brown, Evan. "Discipline of Student for Personal Blog Post Did Not Violate First Amendment." *Journal of Internet Law* 21, no. 3 (September 2008): 12.

Papandrea, Mary-Rose. "Student Speech Rights in the Digital Age." *Florida Law Review* 60, no. 5 (December 2008): 1028–1101.

Tune, Cydney, and Marley Degner. "Blogging and Social Networking: Current Legal Issues." In *Information Technology Law Institute 2008: New Directions: Social Networks, Blogs, Privacy, Mash-Ups, Virtual Worlds and Open Source*, 73–96. New York: Practising Law Institute, 2008.

CHAPTER 6

Do Libel Laws Apply Online?

Case: *I.M.L. v. State of Utah* (2002)

Act: creating a Web site containing negative statements about school officials

Charge: criminal libel; publishing false statements with cruel intent

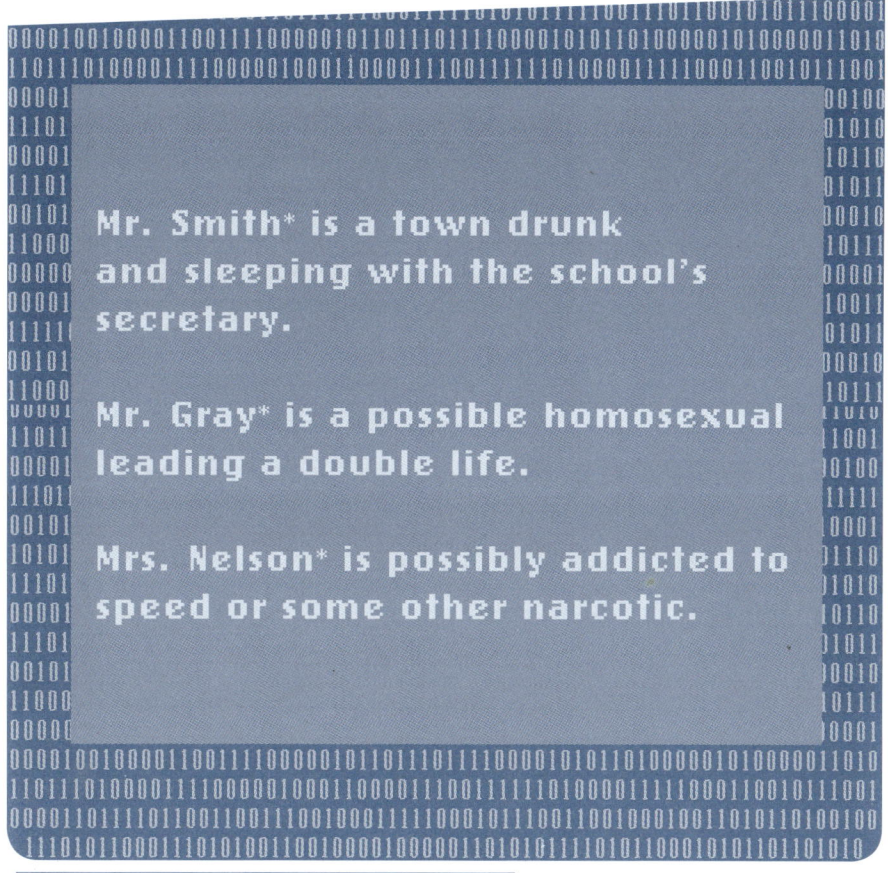

Mr. Smith* is a town drunk and sleeping with the school's secretary.

Mr. Gray* is a possible homosexual leading a double life.

Mrs. Nelson* is possibly addicted to speed or some other narcotic.

* Actual names withheld to protect individuals' privacy.

Ian Michael Lake (I.M.L.) was a 16-year-old junior at Milford High School in Utah in 2000. He had a 3.5 GPA and planned to run for student council. He created a Web site at home declaring the statements on page 71. A friend of Ian's left a note in the computer lab with Ian's Web site address on it. Complaints about the site led to a police investigation during which officers went to Ian's home, interviewed him and his father, and took their computers. The computers were returned after being searched.

Ian told the police he created the site in response to online trash talk about one of his friends. He got carried away and added his comments about the principal and two teachers because he didn't like them. His site contained no threats of violence or reference to any weapons. Ian was arrested and spent seven days in juvenile detention. He was charged with criminal libel in violation of Utah law.

The crime of libel is committed when a written statement is made about someone that exposes him or her to public ridicule or contempt. Courts have consistently ruled that a libelous statement becomes criminal when it's a false statement made with actual malice. Truth is a defense to a libel charge, and the person making the statement must prove its truthfulness.

Utah's 1876 criminal libel statute, which applied to Ian's case, stated that "A person is guilty of libel if he intentionally and with malicious intent to injure another publishes any libel." Ian challenged the state's libel law claiming that it violated free speech. It didn't

> **Civil libel v. Criminal libel**
> All 50 U.S. states have **civil libel** statutes that allow a person to sue in court for damages caused by defamatory statements. Most states do not have **criminal libel** statutes. Where they do exist, the victim must show actual malice by the perpetrator.
>
> Even President Thomas Jefferson favored settling libelous matters in a civil fashion rather than through criminal prosecution. In 1802 he wrote, "I would wish to see the experiment tried of getting along without public prosecution for libels. I believe we can do it. Patience and well-doing, instead of punishment."

require actual malice by the speaker, and it didn't state that truth was a defense to the crime. The state argued that "actual malice" was implied in the law, and that protection for truthful statements already existed, although this was not specified in the statute.

The juvenile court denied Ian's motion to dismiss the charge, and he and his parents appealed the denial to the Utah Supreme Court.

HOW WOULD YOU DECIDE THIS CASE?

Are you surprised that online statements led to criminal charges against Ian? Should truth be a defense to making such statements on the Internet? How would Ian go about proving his statements are true? Even if they *are* true, does that make what he did okay? Do you think the situation could have been handled differently? How? When should school officials take disciplinary action versus calling the police for investigation and prosecution?

WHAT THE COURT DECIDED

The Utah Supreme Court considered the history of libel and defamation laws in the United States dating back to the 1800s. "In this case we consider the application of a law drafted more than one hundred years ago to the most modern of preoccupations—the Internet." The court recognized that the First Amendment never intended to protect intentional falsehoods against innocent private persons. Even if a person spoke out of hatred, the court stated that, "utterances honestly believed contribute to the free interchange of ideas and the ascertainment of truth."

However, in this case, Ian admitted that his statements were false and that he posted them intentionally to expose the faculty to public ridicule. A person that knowingly lies for the express purpose of doing harm to another, as Ian did here, cannot claim protection of the First Amendment. The court stated, "Private citizens such as school administrators and teachers are entitled to be free of such unwarranted, destructive, personal attacks." That said, the court agreed with Ian that Utah's libel statute was overly broad and ambiguous. It was missing essential language regarding actual malice and immunity to truthful statements. The law infringed upon protected speech by punishing statements regardless of the truth or intent of the speaker. Therefore, while Ian's statements were outside the bounds of the First Amendment, the libel law he was accused of breaking was outside the bounds of the Constitution.

The libel charge against Ian was dismissed and Utah's law was declared unconstitutional. The principal then filed a civil lawsuit against Ian and his parents that was settled out of court for several thousand dollars. Because this case raised a First Amendment issue, the court further commented: "To avoid chilling the exercise of vital First Amendment rights, restriction of expression must be expressed in terms which clearly inform citizens of prohibited conduct."

How Does This Decision Affect You?

Your actions may bring unexpected consequences. Ian was not aware that he was breaking the law when he criticized his school principal and teachers, and he had no criminal intent to harm anyone through his writings. Yet consider the outcome of his postings: he spent a week in jail, he had to transfer to a new school in his senior year, his family moved away as a result of community pressure, and he was involved in a civil lawsuit costing his parents additional expense.

You can see from Ian's case that the concept of libel is complicated. It is not easy to define or defend against, and each state has its own law that may apply to you even if you aren't a resident there. Some states' laws carry harsher consequences than others, as apparent in this case. In addition, Ian's case led to a Utah state law being declared unconstitutional, an important result that will affect rulings in the state for years to come.

The bottom line: You may not be as lucky as Ian who was prosecuted under a law judged as defective by the court. You have the right to criticize others, but refrain from hateful attacks and falsehoods.

WHAT IS IAN DOING NOW?

Following his week spent in jail, Ian was released to live with his grandfather and ordered by the judge not to return to Milford, unless he was to appear in court. He graduated the following year from Palm Springs High School in California. His family also left Milford and moved to California.

Ian joined the Army and served a year in Iraq. He is now married and works as an Army recruiter in Arizona. Thinking back, he said, "I should have been punished for what I did—it was dumb—but not charged with a crime." When asked for advice to kids about using the Internet he commented that, "Once you put something out there you can never take it back. No matter how slick you think you are, it can, and probably will be, traced back to you."

> "LIES SERVE NO VALID PUBLIC PURPOSE, AND HAVE NO PROTECTED STATUS IN OUR PUBLIC DISCOURSE."
> —from Ian Lake's court decision

> "FIRST AMENDMENT FREEDOMS NEED BREATHING SPACE TO SURVIVE—GOVERNMENT MAY REGULATE IN THE AREA ONLY WITH NARROW SPECIFICITY."
> —from *NAACP v. Button*, U.S. Supreme Court (1963)

RELATED CASES

Denise E. Finkel v. Facebook & Others (New York, 2009)

Denise Finkel became the target of cyberbullies while she was a junior at Oceanside High School in New York. Four students created a chat group on Facebook called "90 Cents Short of a Dollar" describing Denise as a "woman of dubious morals and dubious sexual character." She was portrayed as an IV drug user who participated in bestiality and who had contracted AIDS.

In March 2009, Denise sued her classmates, their parents, and Facebook for $3 million. She claimed that she was subjected to public hatred, ridicule, and disgrace. Because of the Communications Decency Act of 1996 (see Federal Laws on page 18), Facebook is protected from liability as a service provider for content posted by others. Facebook was dismissed from the lawsuit in September 2009. The lawsuit remains pending against the others at the time of this book's publication.

John Doe, through next friend Laura Cook v. R.C., A.G., K.Z., and M.S. (Illinois, 2009)

In a similar case, four teenagers in Illinois, referred to only as R.C., A.G., K.Z., and M.S., created a fake Facebook profile about an athlete at their school. They included his real name, cell phone number, and numerous photos. They posted sexual statements claiming that he had sex with other males, and comments against President Obama to make him appear racist.

In September 2009, the athlete John Doe* and his mother sued his classmates alleging defamation and severe emotional distress. They seek monetary damages and an order against the four prohibiting them from further attacks. Over 500 people saw the site before Facebook removed it. In addition to humiliation and embarrassment, the student's academic and athletic reputation was damaged, which may affect his future. He and his family were also alienated from many of their friends. The lawsuit remains pending at the time of this book's publication.

Katherine Evans v. Peter Bayer (Florida, 2008)

In November 2007, Katie Evans was an 18-year-old senior at Pembrokes Pines Charter High School in Florida. She was an honor student with no disciplinary record. She was upset with her English teacher, Sarah Phelps, and while at home wrote the following message on her Facebook page:

"Ms. Sarah Phelps is the worst teacher I've ever met! To those select students who have had the displeasure of having Ms. Sarah Phelps, or simply knowing her and her insane antics: Here is the place to express your feelings of hatred."

Katie also added a photo of Ms. Phelps taken from the school yearbook. Three students posted comments supporting Ms. Phelps and criticizing Katie. After two days, Katie voluntarily removed the photo from Facebook. Her teacher didn't see it and Katie remained in her class for the rest of the semester. Eventually word got out about Katie's actions, and two months later the school principal, Peter Bayer, suspended her for three days for cyberbullying and

---

* Actual name withheld to protect individual's privacy.

harassing a staff member. She was pulled from her Advanced Placement classes but graduated on schedule in June 2008, and went on to college at the University of Florida.

In December 2008, Katie filed a lawsuit challenging the suspension as a violation of her freedom of speech. She was concerned about future graduate school and job applications and wanted the school to remove all mention of the suspension from her record. She recognized that being designated a "cyberbully" in an official record would be an obstacle in her life. Her lawsuit remains pending at the time of this book's publication.

Jill Snyder v. Blue Mountain School District (Pennsylvania, 2008)

Eighth-grader Jill Snyder and her boyfriend K.L. created a fake page on MySpace that depicted Jill's principal as a pedophile and sex addict. It included a photo of Principal James McGonigle taken from the school's Web site. They wrote that Mr. McGonigle was a married, bisexual man whose interests included "being a tight ass," "fucking in my office," and "hitting on students and their parents." They designated his Web address as "www.myspace.com/kidsrockmybed."

Both students were suspended for 10 days. Jill filed a suit against the school for the suspension. In September 2008, a federal court upheld the school's suspension stating that it was proper and did not violate her free speech rights. The court followed the *Fraser* decision (see pages 12–13) in authorizing school discipline for elaborate, graphic, and explicit sexual content.

Have You Googled Yourself Lately?
Teachers in England have been advised to google their own names and check social networking sites for offensive material about them. In April 2009, the Education Ministry explained that this is part of their attempt to address cyberbullying and the "shocking level of violence" aimed at schools. Fifteen percent of England's teachers report being the victim of cyberbullying.

THINGS TO THINK ABOUT

Ian accused his principal and teachers of being alcoholics, drug users, unfaithful, and gay. He knew his statements were false, but he still beat the criminal charge of libel. Do you agree with the outcome of Ian's case? The "due process of law" is one of your Constitutional rights under the Fourteenth Amendment and requires that you be notified of any charge filed against you and that criminal laws must be specific and understandable so you know exactly what's prohibited. Even though Ian's statements *were* libelous, the libel law was ambiguous and therefore unconstitutional. What do you think about due process, as applied in Ian's case?

Chapter 6: Further Reading and Resources

Cybertip.ca • cybertip.ca
Canada's national tipline for reporting the online sexual exploitation of children.

National Center for Missing & Exploited Children • www.missingkids.com
This Web site explains how predators can use information and photos posted on social networking profiles to exploit teens. Learn how to think before you post and when to report suspicious online activity.

Carter, Edward L. "Outlaw Speech on the Internet: Examining the Link Between Unique Characteristics of Online Media and Criminal Libel Prosecutions." *Santa Clara Computer and High Technology Law Journal* 21, no. 2 (January 2005): 289–318.

Chemerinsky, Erwin. "Students Do Leave Their First Amendment Rights at the Schoolhouse Gates: What's Left of *Tinker*?" *Drake Law Review* 48, no. 3 (2000): 527–546.

CHAPTER 7

Litigating Lewdness

Case: *Gregory Requa v. Kent School District (2007)*

Act: placing a link on his MySpace profile page to a video of his teacher, along with critical comments

Charge: creating a lewd and offensive video of a teacher in the classroom

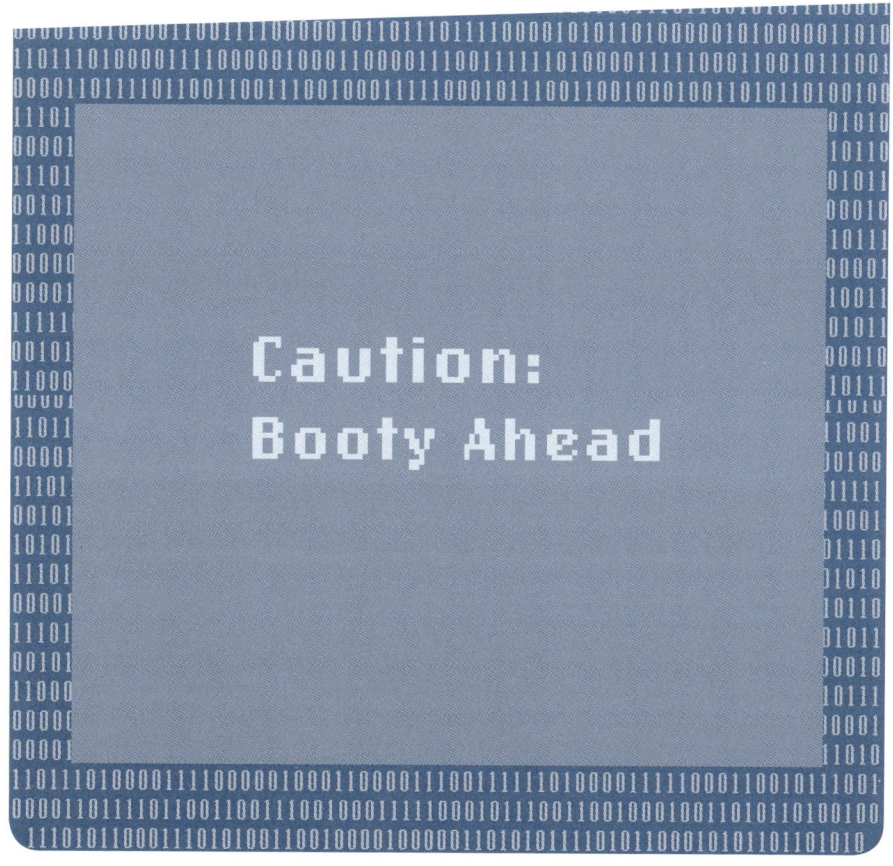

The previous text was the caption on a cell phone video filmed at Kentridge High School in Washington in June 2006. A student (identified only as S.W.) admitted to doing the filming in English class. Greg Requa was a junior in the class and admitted to linking the video that had been posted on YouTube to his MySpace page. Although other students stated otherwise, Greg denied any involvement with filming, editing, or posting the video on YouTube. Greg had never been in trouble before, and carried a 2.97 GPA. He had also won a DECA (Delta Epsilon Chi Association) competition and was set to compete at the state level.

The video was taken without the teacher's knowledge or permission. It included shots of her rear as she walked and as she was bending over. Greg allegedly added the graphics and a musical soundtrack, along with comments about her hygiene and teaching methods. One shot featured a third student standing behind her making faces and pelvic thrusts in her direction. S.W. told the principal, "All I did was some filming. Greg did editing and posted it online."

A local Seattle news channel discovered the video while investigating a story about student postings on YouTube. The reporter contacted Kentridge High for comment and aired a story including Greg's video in 2007. Greg removed the link from his MySpace page when he learned of the news coverage. This was the first time the teacher learned of the video. The school imposed a 40-day suspension on the students, which would be cut in half if each student completed a research paper while suspended.

Greg and his parents appealed the discipline to the School Board. A hearing was conducted and the Board determined "that Greg's denial of his involvement is not credible." Greg claimed that his alleged involvement was a rumor based on his reputation as a skilled video editor. The Board found that Greg's acts constituted sexual harassment in violation of school policy and upheld the suspension.

Greg took the matter to the Washington Western District Court, arguing that even if it could be proved that he was involved in the production and posting of the video, it was protected speech. He further asserted that the suspension jeopardized his graduation since the suspension ran right up to the end of the school year. The school maintained that Greg was disciplined for his conduct (creating an unauthorized video of a teacher in class) and *not* for his speech (the off-campus editing and posting of the video).

HOW WOULD YOU DECIDE THIS CASE?

Throughout these proceedings, Greg maintained his position that he did nothing but link the YouTube video to his MySpace page. What do you think? How much weight should be given to the statements of other students? What about S.W.'s claim that he filmed the video, but that Greg did the rest and was essentially the video's "director"? Does the content of the video offend you? Should teachers and administrators expect some privacy, or is everything fair game to be broadcast worldwide? Should Greg's academic record be considered in determining an appropriate consequence?

WHAT THE COURT DECIDED

The district court agreed with the school that the primary issue was not the editing and posting of the video off campus, but the initial creation of the video. It was the unauthorized shooting and subject matter that violated school policy. The suspension was not for the purpose of regulating off-campus speech.

Although Greg argued that the entire video was merely criticism of a teacher, the court disagreed. "Footage of her buttocks, a pelvic thrust... graphics and a 'booty' rap song cannot be denominated as anything other than lewd and offensive," said the court.

The court then weighed the harm to Greg if the suspension was not lifted. It considered the loss of a full-time, in-class education, and the experiences enjoyed in the final months of high school. It also weighed the harm to the school if the court set the suspension aside. "The deterrent impact of the consequences meted out for the violations of the student code will be lost—sanctions are meant to communicate." The court found that the school's interests outweighed Greg's. He could minimize the punishment by writing the paper and completing the 20-day suspension before graduation, as the cameraman, S.W., chose to do.

How Does This Decision Affect You?

Some of the cases presented here are a mix of student activity at school with additional work at home. It may be impossible to determine exact percentages of each, so courts use a "totality of circumstances" test. In Greg's case, breaking a school rule paired with the nature of the violation supported his suspension. The U.S. Supreme Court has yet to address school discipline for off-campus Internet activity. Because courts across the nation differ in these cases, it won't be long before the issue is ripe for Supreme Court review.

> "THE PUBLIC HAS AN INTEREST IN CLASSROOMS IN WHICH TEACHERS CAN WORK FREE OF HARASSMENT, LEWDNESS, AND INAPPROPRIATE BEHAVIOR."
>
> "A STUDENT'S RIGHT TO CRITICIZE HIS OR HER TEACHERS IS A RIGHT SECURED BY THE CONSTITUTION. A SCHOOL DISTRICT'S INTEREST IN MAINTAINING AN ENVIRONMENT THAT IS HELPFUL AND NOT HARMFUL TO LEARNING IS ALSO IMPORTANT."
>
> —both quotes are from Gregory Requa's court decision

The bottom line: Consider the bigger picture of how your behavior might be interpreted. Even if your actions are not considered lewd or did not all take place on school grounds, when taken as a whole, they still may be grounds for discipline. Keep in mind there are still "gray areas" in the law.

What Is Greg Doing Now?

Greg graduated with his class and started college at Full Sail University in Florida, studying digital arts and design. When interviewed in 2008, he offered the following advice to teens: "Don't fall victim to peer pressure, it will usually make you end up hating what you did. And if that someone is pressuring you too hard, then you should re-think your friendship with them."

Cell Phone Crackdowns Around the World

The City of **New York** school system banned cell phones at school in 2005. Parents objecting to the ban challenged it in court, but the ban was upheld. The court ruled that the ban was reasonable because cell phones can be disruptive and have been used by kids to cheat on tests, take pictures and videos in locker rooms, crank call teachers, and gather buddies during fights.

In 2008, the government of **Japan** asked parents to monitor and limit their kids' use of cell phones in an attempt to protect elementary and junior high students from cyber-criminals. They also requested manufacturers to make cell phones with only the talking function and GPS for the child's safety.

The island country of **Cyprus** has also cracked down on cell phones at school. Incidents of cell phone videos posted on the Web and texting during class and exams led to new laws in 2008. Students caught with a cell phone at school could be suspended, and anyone caught filming could be expelled.

In January 2009, the Education Ministry of the **Czech Republic** began allowing school headmasters to discipline students who use cell phones to film other students being bullied or who attempt to blackmail teachers by posting videos of them online. Repeat offenders may be referred to the police.

RELATED CASES: TEACHERS ON FILM

Logan Glover v. Lafayette High School (Missouri, 2008)

Fifteen-year-old Logan Glover used a digital camera to take pictures of his language arts teacher in class. The teacher, Jessica Hauser, did not know she was being photographed. While Logan was photographing, two other students stood near Ms. Hauser, posing and acting out. Logan posted the photos on his Facebook profile, and some of the students printed them and brought them to school. The photos were not demeaning or embarrassing and were posted without comment or names. However, Ms. Hauser was upset that her trust had been violated and she felt disrespected.

Two weeks later, the assistant principal called Logan to her office and searched his cell phone for the photos. When she didn't find them, she asked Logan for copies. He gave her all copies and then deleted them from Facebook. Logan admitted that he took and posted the pictures online. He was removed from the class and given a three-day out-of-school suspension for disrupting the class by having the other kids posing for the camera and being off-task. Those kids were given three days of in-school suspension.

In December 2007, Logan and his father sued the school district for punishing him for his off-campus protected expression. They claimed that he was suspended simply for posting the pictures and that there was no disturbance at school or in Ms. Hauser's class. The school argued that the case was about controlling classroom behavior and not about Logan's right to communicate online. In August 2008, Logan and the school district reached an undisclosed settlement and the case was dismissed.

Vesikko (Finland, 2007)

High school student Toni Vesikko was at a school party in 2007, where he used his cell phone to film his teacher singing karaoke. He posted the video on YouTube and wrote under the picture that she was a lunatic singing at a mental hospital. In the first case of its kind in Finland, Toni was found guilty of "intentional defamation." His teacher suffered anxiety and depression from the incident. Toni was ordered to pay $4,000 in fines, court costs, and damages for causing his teacher to suffer.

RELATED CASES: LEWDNESS AND OBSCENITY

State v. Dougherty (Iowa, 2008)

Andy Dougherty of Iowa was 17 when he made a 10-second cell phone video of himself with his pants down fooling around with his teenage girlfriend. After they broke up, he sought revenge because she was spreading rumors about him. Andy sent the video to a 17-year-old friend and the police discovered it. Andy was charged with a sex crime: telephone dissemination of obscene material to a minor. The possible penalties included two years in jail and 10 years as a registered sex offender.

In August 2008, Andy pleaded guilty to three counts of harassment, which were lesser crimes. He was sentenced to 20 days in jail, 100 hours of community service, and a $300 fine. If he had been convicted of the sex crime, he would not have been allowed to live on campus at any college, and he may have been prevented from becoming a teacher, doctor, and other professional positions.

State v. Alpert (Florida, 2008)

After breaking up with his 16-year-old girlfriend, 18-year-old Phillip Alpert sent a nude picture of her to over 70 people, including her parents, grandparents, and teachers. Phillip was charged with sending child pornography and was convicted. He was sentenced to five years probation, and required to register as a sex offender until his 43rd birthday.

Interviewed in 2009, Phillip stated, "A lot of my friends have not stood by me . . . people don't want to talk to me anymore." He is required to attend sex offender meetings and is having trouble finding a job.

Miller v. Skumanick (Pennsylvania, 2009)

Marissa Miller, age 13, attended a slumber party with her girlfriends. They took cell phone pictures of each other including one of Marissa and another girl from the waist up wearing their bras. A separate photo showed a girl with a bath towel wrapped around her body beneath her breasts. Two years later, a school administrator saw the pictures on a confiscated cell phone and notified the police.

The Pennsylvania district attorney made the same offer to Marissa and her friends that had been extended to other students caught "sexting." To avoid being charged with child pornography, they had to complete an education program about sexual violence and pornography, and submit to random drug testing.

The girls and their parents thought the offer was unfair and illegal. In March 2009, they filed a lawsuit in federal court against the prosecutor asking the court for an order preventing him from filing criminal charges against the girls. The court ruled that the girls' lawsuit had merit and therefore ordered the district attorney not to file any charges against them based on the photos.

STORIES OF SEXTING

In March 2009, a 14-year-old girl in New Jersey was charged with possession and distribution of child pornography. She uploaded 30 photos of herself to her MySpace profile for her boyfriend to see. She was arrested and released to her mother. She faced 17 years in prison and sex offender registration if convicted. She reached an agreement with the state and was placed on six months probation and counseling in exchange for dismissal of the charges upon completion. Other states taking action against teens posting sexually explicit material include Connecticut, North Dakota, Ohio, Utah, Vermont, Virginia, and Wisconsin.

In January 2009, three girls at Salem High School in Pennsylvania were charged with disseminating child pornography. The girls, ages 14 and 15, sent text messages including nude pictures of themselves to three boys, ages 16 and 17. The boys were charged with possession of child pornography. The pictures were discovered by a school administrator who took a cell phone from one of the girls who had it on in class. All of the teens accepted a lesser misdemeanor charge and were sentenced to community service hours and education classes.

> **Sexual Texting = Sexting**
>
> A popular flirting technique among teens involves the posting of nude photos of yourself or others on the Internet or in a text message ("sexting"). Whether sent to a boyfriend, girlfriend, or a private list of friends, these photos can easily be forwarded, printed, and distributed for worldwide Internet viewing. Some teens have faced criminal charges for their postings, including contributing to the delinquency of a minor, child pornography, and harassment.
>
> - 22% of cell phone users ages 13–17 report they've posted or sent naked or semi-naked photos/videos of themselves, mostly for fun or to be flirtatious.
> - Roughly one in seven kids online (10- to 17-year-olds) received a sexual solicitation or approach over the Internet. Four percent of the same group received an aggressive sexual solicitation.

> "WE TEND TO FEEL THAT BECAUSE IT'S ELECTRONIC AND SLIPS INTO THE ETHER THAT IT'S SOMEHOW IMPERMANENT OR UNREAL. BUT THE OPPOSITE IS TRUE. NOT ONLY IS IT PERMANENT, BUT IT'S EASILY REPLICABLE. THIS ISN'T CAMP WITH A COPY OF PLAYBOY AND SHOWING TWO OR THREE FRIENDS. IT'S POTENTIALLY GLOBAL."
> —Professor Steve Jones, University of Illinois at Chicago

In 2009, a 15-year-old Nebraska freshman was placed on one-year probation for sending a nude picture of himself to a 13-year-old girl. He was charged with distributing obscene material and pled guilty. He was also ordered into counseling, given 20 community service hours, restricted from contacting the victim, and prohibited from using a cell phone while on probation.

A 15-year-old girl in Ohio was arrested in 2008 and charged with child pornography. She sent nude cell phone pictures of herself to classmates. A 17-year-old Wisconsin boy posted nude photos of his 16-year-old ex-girlfriend that she sent him when they were together. He was charged with child pornography and sexual exploitation of a child.

Jessica Logan was an 18-year-old senior at Sycamore High School in Ohio. She sent her boyfriend nude cell phone pictures of herself. After they broke up, he sent them to hundreds of students in several schools. Jessica was harassed and taunted at school, called a whore and a slut. This led to depression and missed school days. Two months later, in July 2008, Jessica hanged herself in her bedroom. Her mother, Cynthia, is now speaking out about the dangers of sexting and supporting legislation addressing electronic communication by tweens and teens.

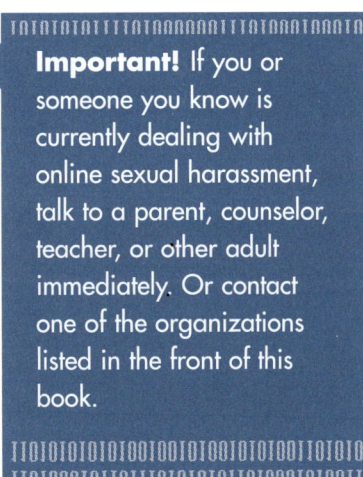

Important! If you or someone you know is currently dealing with online sexual harassment, talk to a parent, counselor, teacher, or other adult immediately. Or contact one of the organizations listed in the front of this book.

The following poem was written by Jessica Logan at age 17, a year before her suicide. It is reprinted here with permission from her mother.

> The door that lies before you
>
> Offers opportunity, hope, and a prosperous future
>
> The door does not promise anything,
>
> Only you can ensure your own destiny
>
> The door that stands before you is a decision,
>
> Symbolic to your future and past
>
> What has happened?
>
> What is yet to happen?
>
> And the present time you are in.
>
> Crossing through can have great risk,
>
> But with great risk comes great reward.
>
> If you do not risk you do not gain nor lose anything
>
> You are untainted by knowledge of
>
> what lies beyond your present life.
>
> The door itself
>
> Makes no promises
>
> It is only a door

Jessica Logan

In a case similar to Jessica's, Florida middle school student Hope Witsell sent a topless photo of herself to a boy she liked. The text was intercepted by another student using the boy's cell phone, and the photo spread to other schools. Hope was grounded by her parents over the summer and suspended for the first week of school. She endured months of taunting, including comments like, "Here comes the slut." On September 12, 2009, she hung herself from the canopy of her bed with a pink scarf. She was 13 years old.

THINGS TO THINK ABOUT

As you know from chapter 5 (Avery Doninger's case), the Family Educational Rights and Privacy Act provides you with privacy rights as a student. The law is very specific about what information about you may be released. Why do you think this is important? Should your teachers and school officials have similar protections? Why or why not? Since no specific law shields teachers from being secretly photographed or filmed, what role does common decency and respect play?

Reminders for Avoiding Sexting

- Don't assume anything you send or post is going to remain private.
- There is no changing your mind in cyberspace—anything you post will never go away.
- Don't be pressured into doing something that makes you uncomfortable, even in cyberspace.
- Consider the recipient's reaction before you send.
- Nothing is truly anonymous.
- If you are a minor, it may be a felony to take nude pictures of yourself and send them out online or by cell phone.
- Keep in mind that a dumb moment can last a lifetime in cyberspace. What starts out as harmless fun may have serious consequences.

Chapter 7: Further Reading and Resources

That's Not Cool • www.thatsnotcool.com
Get advice from other teens on how to deal with textual harassment, pic pressure, constant messaging, and more. Is someone pressuring or harassing you? Tell them to back off by sending a callout card.

Chaffin, Stacy M. "The New Playground Bullies of Cyberspace: Online Peer Sexual Harassment." *Howard Law Journal* 51, no. 3 (Spring 2008): 773–818.

Conn, Kathleen, and Kevin P. Brady. "MySpace and Its Relatives: The Cyberbullying Dilemma." *West's Education Law Reporter* 226 (January 2008): 1.

Sanchez Abril, Patricia. "A (My)Space of One's Own: On Privacy and Online Social Networks." *Northwestern Journal of Technology and Internet Property* 6, no. 1 (Fall 2007): 73–88.

CHAPTER 8

What's the Issue— Content or Access?

Case: *Jon Coy v. Canton City Schools* (2002)

Act: using a school computer to access his personal Web site that the school deemed profane

Charge: unauthorized use of school property, online profanity, and disobedience

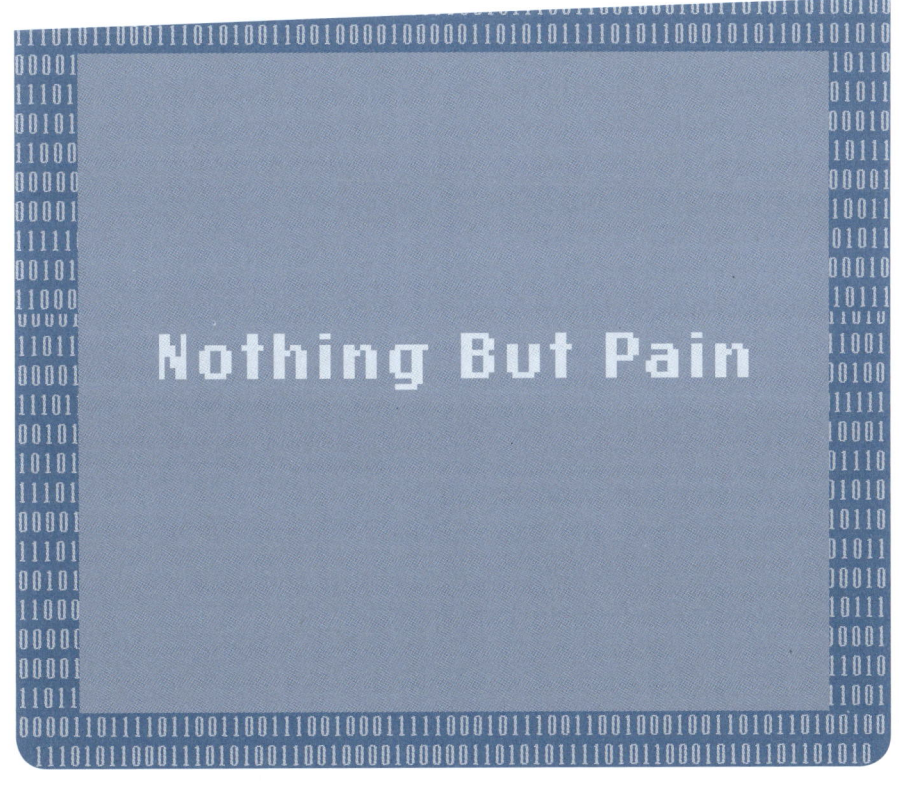

Jon Coy was 14 years old and in 8th grade at North Canton Middle School in Ohio. In early 2001, he and his friends made a video called "Nothing But Pain" about their exploits that included rollerblading, skateboarding, skits, and daring stunts.

Jon created a Web site to promote his video, and did not name his school or any school official on it. The site contained pictures of Jon and his friends with some biographical information and quotes. It also included a section called "losers" that featured three boys who went to his school, with insults written under each picture. One described a boy as being sexually aroused by his mother, while another displayed a boy giving the "finger." There was also some profanity and, as the court stated, "a depressingly high number of spelling and grammatical errors." (*Note:* This was merely an observation, of course—Jon was not legally judged based on his spelling!)

Like many schools in the United States, North Canton had an Internet policy (an "AUP") that Jon and his parents signed at the beginning of the school year. The policy authorized acceptable behavior for students using the school's computers. It prohibited students from hacking into unauthorized computers, Web sites, or information databases, and displaying offensive messages or pictures. Students were warned of disciplinary action for violating the policy.

> **What's an AUP?**
> Many middle and high schools have an AUP, "Acceptable Use Policy," regarding the Internet. It covers what a student can and cannot access while in school. The policy and explanation of use should be in your student handbook.

Word about Jon's site spread at school and eventually the principal learned of it. However, he didn't take any action until Jon was caught accessing his Web site from a school computer. Jon was suspended for four days for unauthorized computer use, online profanity, and disobedience. He was also referred to the school superintendent for possible expulsion. The police were notified and Jon and his parents were interviewed at home.

The school district held a hearing and expelled Jon for 80 days. This decision was later modified to allow Jon to continue in school on probation status, but he was restricted from participating in any after-school activities. Jon and his parents disagreed with the school's response to the Web site and challenged it in court. They claimed that Jon's freedom of speech was violated and that the school's Internet policy was vague. The school responded by categorizing his Web site as "lewd and vulgar" and therefore not protected speech. They further stated that Jon was punished for accessing his site at school, not because of the site's content.

HOW WOULD YOU DECIDE THIS CASE?

Do you think Jon's Web site was obscene? Did it cross the line of appropriate expression? Do you think it disrupted any classes or violated anyone's personal rights? Should the school punish Jon for his sexual comments or calling someone a loser? What about for accessing the site at school, which violated the school's code of conduct? Was an 80-day probation period a fair consequence or do you think the original four-day suspension was sufficient?

WHAT THE COURT DECIDED

The school maintained that the punishment was justified because Jon violated the Internet use policy by accessing his Web site on a school computer. However, it was not clear from the evidence presented to the court whether he was disciplined because of unauthorized access or because of his site's content. The court stated that if the school disciplined Jon "purely because they did not like what was contained in his personal Web site," then Jon would win unless the school could show that it caused a disturbance on campus.

The appellate court sent the case back for trial so a jury could decide which was the deciding issue: content or access. On the question of obscene content, the court held that "While somewhat crude and juvenile, the Web site contains no material that could remotely be considered obscene." Before a jury heard Jon's case, the parties reached an agreement. The school agreed to remove the incident from Jon's record and pay him $20,000, part of which paid his legal fees.

How Does This Decision Affect You?

Courts are not in the business of running schools. They do not want to be involved in the day-to-day affairs of education. Conduct codes spelled out in student handbooks exist for a reason and carry consequences for violation (see chapter 13 for more on this topic). The simple act of accessing an unauthorized Web site may be cause for discipline, regardless of the content of the site. As you see in Jon's case, there is a difference between content and access. Jon's school was not able to prove that his punishment was in response solely to unauthorized access, and so Jon won his case. However, he faced distressing consequences along the way—he was suspended, interviewed by police, put on probation status at school, and involved in an extended court battle.

> "THE FIRST AMENDMENT IS THERE FOR THE MINORITY, NOT THE MAJORITY, WHO WILL SAY THINGS THAT ARE NOT POLITICALLY CORRECT."
> —James Madison, U.S. president, 1809–1817
>
> "I DISAPPROVE OF WHAT YOU SAY, BUT I WILL DEFEND TO THE DEATH YOUR RIGHT TO SAY IT."
> —Voltaire (18th-century French philosopher)

The bottom line: Whether or not you read your school's code of conduct, it applies to you as a student. Ignorance is not a defense for breaking a rule. It's safe to assume that personal use of a school's computer is a violation, and there will likely be penalties—with or without profane content.

WHAT IS JON DOING NOW?

Jon attends Kent State University in Ohio studying English and sociology. He also freelances as a videographer and filmmaker.

In 2008, 21-year-old Jon commented about Internet and cell phone use. He said, "Teens and even younger children need to become aware of the consequences from their improper use. Be careful of what you say and type—if what you're saying to someone could potentially cause harm or distress, think about holding it back."

RELATED CASES

Christopher Bowler v. Hudson High School (Massachusetts, 2004)

In 2004, senior Christopher Bowler started an organization at Hudson High School in Massachusetts "where students could feel comfortable expressing their opinions." He put up 10 posters at school advertising the first meeting of the Conservative Club. The poster included the address of a Web site that had links to videos of jihadist beheadings of Americans in the Middle East. The school was concerned about exposing its students to such gruesome and graphic images. School officials blocked access to the site and ordered Christopher to take down the posters. He was later allowed to hang the posters with the Web site marked out.

Christopher sued the school district as well as school administrators for violating his First Amendment rights. After three years of litigation, the case was settled on the eve of trial in 2008. The school agreed to amend its policy to forbid censorship of student expression based on political viewpoints. Christopher stated he was "glad that the administration has finally recognized that if this school is going to pride itself on a democratic environment that emphasizes free speech, that includes all viewpoints." Although this case is about school censorship of political speech, it demonstrates a subtle form of cyberbullying. Displaying a link or reference to violent or threatening material may be used to send bullying messages. In Christopher's case, the Web site listed on his poster was ruled to be political speech and not cyberbullying, but the distinction was a subtle one. Similar cases might result in a different ruling.

Cyberbullying on the Rise

Many schools, including Jon's, are implementing AUPs and other measures to control student Internet use. Threats, harassment, and bullying by way of text messaging, email, and social networking sites have rapidly expanded across the globe. Online taunts are increasingly leading to school yard face-offs. Gang posturing on MySpace and Facebook has led to school fights and shootings. Consider the following facts:

- Online harassment of American kids ages 10 to 17 increased 50% from 2000 to 2005. The number of young people who said they had made rude or nasty comments to someone on the Internet increased from 14% to 28% in the same period.

- 25% of Canadian students surveyed in 2009 reported being bullied in the past few months. A survey of young people in Canada showed that 70% of those who have bullied someone online thought they would never get caught, and that they bully because it's "cool."

- In Australia, 94% of students experience cell phone bullying at some point. Boys are more often the target of offensive text messages and pornographic images, but more girls are psychologically affected.

- 1 in 3 teens is victimized by cyberbullying in England.

Safety Tips for Dealing with Cyberbullies

If you are being harassed online:

- Never reply to harassing messages.

- Save all harassing messages to show your parents and send to your Internet service provider.

- Walk away from the computer—don't prolong the harassment.

- Tell a parent or another trusted adult immediately.

State v. McInerney (California, 2008)

Larry King was 15 and in 8th grade at E.O. Green Junior High in California. He had professed to a friend that he was gay and began cross-dressing and wearing makeup to class. Larry was bullied at school, and some of his teachers tried to help him. Girls at school used cell phones to take his picture when he dressed up, and they shared the photos online with classmates.

Larry had allegedly embarrassed 14-year-old classmate Brandon McInerney by flirting with him at school. One day, while in class, Brandon stood up, pointed a gun at Larry, and shot him twice. Larry died two days later. Brandon was arrested and charged with first-degree murder and committing a hate crime. Tried as an adult, Brandon faces the possibility of life in prison. The decision remains pending at the time of this book's publication.

On the one-year anniversary of the shooting, February 12, 2009, the U.S. Congress filed a Resolution calling for education to help students respect each other's differences and for laws against name-calling and bullying.

THINGS TO THINK ABOUT

Are you aware of the debate about Internet and cell phone access at school? Do you know what your school rules are? School officials work toward a balance of respecting your rights and maintaining a safe educational environment without disruption. In your opinion, are your school's rules reasonable, or should students be trusted to decide what's "acceptable use" on campus? Do you agree with your school's restrictions on accessing unauthorized Web sites? Why or why not?

Chapter 8: Further Reading and Resources

BeatBullying • www.beatbullying.org
BeatBullying is an international bullying prevention charity campaigning to make bullying unacceptable. You will find peer chat, news, and mentoring with counselors.

Cybersmart • www.cybersmart.gov.au
The Cybersmart program is a national cybersafety education program in Australia.

Internet Crime Complaint Center • www.ic3.gov
Have you or someone you know been a victim of an Internet related crime? File a complaint at this government Web site, a collaborative effort with the FBI. After being reviewed, complaints are referred to law enforcement agencies.

SchoolTipline • www.schooltipline.com
If your school has this service, you can anonymously report bullying, sexual harassment, vandalism, discrimination, and drug use at school. It's available 24/7 and designated school officials receive your report immediately.

Teens Against Bullying • www.teensagainstbullying.org
Sponsored by the Pacer Center in Minneapolis, Minnesota, this edgy educational resource is designed to empower teens in dealing with bullying situations.

Calvert, Clay. "Off-Campus Speech, On-Campus Punishment: Censorship of the Emerging Internet Underground." *Boston University Journal of Science and Technology Law* 7, no. 2 (2001): 244–285.

Rutherford, Sally. "Kids Surfing the Net at School: What Are the Legal Issues?" *Rutgers Computer and Technology Law Journal* 24, no. 2 (1998): 417–451.

CHAPTER 9

Free Speech or True Threat?

Case: *Joshua Mahaffey v. Waterford School District* (2002)

Act: creating a Web site with offensive content

Charge: issuing threats against students and disrupting school

---

SATAN'S MISSION FOR YOU THIS WEEK:

Stab someone for no reason then set them on fire throw them off of a cliff, watch them suffer and with their last breath, just before everything goes black, spit on their face. Killing people is wrong don't do it unless I'm there to watch.

PS: NOW THAT YOU'VE READ MY WEB PAGE PLEASE DON'T GO KILLING PEOPLE AND STUFF THEN BLAMING IT ON ME, OK?

Joshua Mahaffey was 15 when he and a friend created this Web site in 2001. They were students at Waterford Kettering High School in Michigan. They called it "Satan's Web page" and, according to Joshua, wrote it for laughs because they were bored.

The site informed readers, "This site has no purpose. It is here to say what is cool, and what sucks. For example, Music is cool. School sucks. I hope you enjoy the page." The Web site then listed "people I wish would die," which included names of several students.

A parent notified the police about the site. Joshua was interviewed and admitted to contributing to it and that some of the content may have been added on a school computer. However, there was no investigation into whether school property was used. No criminal charges were filed against Joshua. At the encouragement of the police and the school, Joshua's parents placed him in a local psychiatric hospital. After three days, the doctors reported that he was not a danger to himself or others, and recommended that he return to school. At this point, the school suspended him for the first semester (a total of 143 days).

Joshua and his parents sued the school district for violating his freedom of expression. They argued that his off-campus speech was protected and that the school could not punish him for it. The school claimed that they could discipline students for off-campus conduct if the school rule was reasonable and the conduct had some effect on the school.

HOW WOULD YOU DECIDE THIS CASE?

What do you think led to Joshua's suspension? Was it the phrase "people I wish would die" followed by a list of students' names? Or was the graphic "Satan's Mission" statement the key issue for Joshua's Web site? What about Joshua's right to free speech and his note warning others "not to go killing people"? Were his comments truly disruptive or a serious threat to anyone? How would you feel if your name was on his list?

WHAT THE COURT DECIDED

After a review of applicable case law, the court determined that Joshua's comments on "Satan's Web Page" did not substantially interfere with the educational process of Waterford High School. There was no evidence of any disruption or that the rights of any students were violated.

The court then considered the school's position that Joshua's online speech constituted threats. A true threat is defined as "a statement communicated as a serious expression of an intention to inflict bodily harm upon or take the life of a person." In this case, there was no evidence that Joshua sent his statements to anyone, including the listed students. The court noted that following the mission statement was the warning not to "go killing people." Therefore Joshua's statements were protected speech.

> **True threat:** a statement communicated as a serious expression of an intention to inflict bodily harm upon or take the life of another person.

Next, the court considered the length of his suspension and stated: "A short suspension is, of course, a far milder deprivation than expulsion. But education is perhaps the most important function of state and local governments, and the total exclusion from the educational process for more than a trivial period is a serious event in the life of the suspended child." The court ruled that the semester-long suspension was inappropriate because Joshua wasn't allowed to have a lawyer at the hearing or present his own witnesses.

HOW DOES THIS DECISION AFFECT YOU?

Although Joshua ultimately won his case against the school district, one thing you can learn from his yearlong ordeal: anytime you say or do something that is viewed as a violation, there may be immediate consequences. You might challenge the punishment—which is your right—but rarely do you receive immediate relief. Appealing to the school board may take several weeks, and taking the matter to court can take several years. In this case, Joshua brought upon himself a three-day hospitalization including a mental health evaluation. He also lost a semester at school since the court didn't decide his case until a year after the incident.

> *The bottom line:* Even if you "win" your argument in the end, your actions could still result in losses that cannot be undone.

WHAT IS JOSHUA DOING NOW?

Joshua didn't return to Waterford High School. He went to a neighboring school district, skipped 11th grade, and graduated in 2002.

> "TECHNOLOGY CAN HELP ADOLESCENTS NAVIGATE THROUGH PERIODS OF ANGST AND INSECURITY. ONLINE COMMUNICATION WITH EVEN AN UNKNOWN PEER CAN ALLEVIATE THE TEMPORARY STRESS OF FEELING REJECTION. THE ONLINE WORLD ENABLES KIDS TO CONNECT EVEN FROM THAT LONELY BEDROOM AT HOME."
> —Jaana Juvonen, UCLA professor

Teen Internet Addiction

Joshua and his friend claimed they created their Web site out of boredom. For some teens, boredom along with stress and loneliness can lead to an Internet addiction. Teen Internet addiction has been identified as a serious problem in the United States, South Korea, China, and Taiwan. One estimate puts the number at 9 million Americans at risk for the disorder.

In a study of 9,400 Taiwanese teenagers, researchers found that those with signs of Internet addiction said they had hit, shoved, or threatened someone in the past year. A preoccupation with online chatting, gaming, and adult forums showed a link to aggressive behavior.

RELATED CASES

Keeley Houghton, Worcester Crown Court (England, 2009)

Believed to be the first person jailed for threatening messages on a social networking site, Keeley Houghton of England, age 18, was sentenced in August 2009 to three months in a young offenders' institution. She pleaded guilty to online harassment of Emily Moore, also 18. This wasn't the first time Keeley had a run in with Emily. In 2005, she was convicted of assaulting Emily as she walked home from school. Keeley was expelled from school and two years later she was convicted of criminal damage for kicking Emily's front door.

Internet Rescue Boot Camp

South Korea has developed the Jump Up Internet Rescue School, a 12-day boot camp to counter Internet addiction that includes rigorous physical exercise and group activities. The goal is to build emotional connections to the real world, and it is believed to be the first program of its kind.

In an extreme case of Internet addiction, 15-year-old Hughstan Schlicker shot and killed his father at home in Mesa, Arizona, in February 2008. After calling the police, he shot the computer. He told detectives that he used the Internet to talk with his friends and that two of them helped him when he tried to commit suicide a few weeks earlier. When his parents discovered that he was talking online about killing himself, they took away his computer. Hughstan, who had spent hours every day on MySpace, now felt cut off from his world. Losing the computer was "like I was stabbed with a knife," he said in explanation of the shooting. He was arrested and charged with first-degree murder. In 2009, Hughstan pleaded guilty to second-degree murder and was sentenced to 20 years in prison.

Then in July 2009, Keeley threatened Emily at a pub. Two days later, Keeley wrote on her own Facebook page that she was "going to murder the bitch." In sentencing Keeley, the judge stated, "Bullies are by their nature cowards, in school and society. The evil, odious effects of being bullied stay with you for life." Keeley was also ordered to have no contact, including by Internet, with Emily for the next five years.

In the Matter of 21 Students (California, 2006)

I hate Deborah*

This was the heading on a California middle school student's MySpace page, along with an anti-Semitic reference. In 2006 he posted the message, "Who here wants to take a shotgun and blast her in the head over a thousand times?" A teacher discovered the threatening post while browsing MySpace, and the student was suspended and faced expulsion proceedings. Police investigated the matter as a hate crime. Concerned with school safety, 20 of the boy's classmates at TeWinkle Middle School who viewed the posting were also suspended for two days. Some parents called the school's response to the viewers an "extreme reaction," since the posting was made on a personal computer, at home, and after school hours. The school explained that they could discipline the students because their primary connection as a group was the school, and their behavior presented a danger to the school community.

In the Matter of Brian Conradt (Indiana, 1999)

At Indiana's Carmel High School, Brian Conradt referred to 11 teachers and administrators as "Satan worshipping demons." His Web site "tyme-2-dye" included satanic symbols and urged fellow students to laugh at and tease the named teachers. The school's initials, CHS, were used to spell "Come Hail Satan."

Brian was suspended for five days and required to write the teachers an apology. He claimed he meant it only as a joke, but

---
*Actual name of student withheld to protect her privacy.

decided to shut down his Web site. No charges were filed against Brian, but three teachers sued him for making false statements that caused them mental suffering and humiliation. One teacher considered his comments threatening and scary. "It was not at all humorous . . . the flaming pentagrams and stuff about shunning us is not funny to me," she said.

Brian transferred to a private school in Colorado after the incident. The lawsuit was settled for $5,000, which was the state's limit on a parent's liability for the acts of a child. Brian now works as a Web designer for a digital media company.

THINGS TO THINK ABOUT

How much time do you typically spend online every day? Do you think teens who spend a lot of time online are more likely to commit acts of cyberbullying like the ones described in this chapter? Did you know there was such a phenomenon as an addiction to the Internet? Do you know someone who may fit this description? The cure is obvious, but like any addiction, difficult to achieve. What could you do to help? Your influence on your peers may be more successful than lectures or reprimands from adults.

Internet Use Safety Tips

- Limit your time online. Maintain a healthy balance between real-life friends, family, school, work, and the virtual world.

- Protect your password and limit your friend list to those you know.

- Think before you click. What you post online is there forever.

- Don't post a photo of yourself unless you're prepared to attach it to a job, college, or scholarship application.

- Protect your friends' privacy. Get their okay before posting their pictures.

- Use caution when corresponding with people online. They may not be who they say they are.

Chapter 9: Further Reading and Resources

Calvert, Clay, and Robert D. Richards. "Columbine Fallout: The Long-Term Effects on Free Expression Take Hold in Public Schools." *Boston University Law Review* 83, no. 5 (2003): 1089–1140.

Kosse, Susan. "Student Designed Home Web Pages: Does Title IX or the First Amendment Apply?" *Arizona Law Review* 43, no. 4 (2001): 905–930.

CHAPTER 10

When Creative Writing Becomes Criminal Content

Case: *Nick Emmett v. Kent School District* (2000)

Act: creating an unofficial school home page with fake obituaries for students

Charge: harassment, intimidation, and disruption of school's educational process

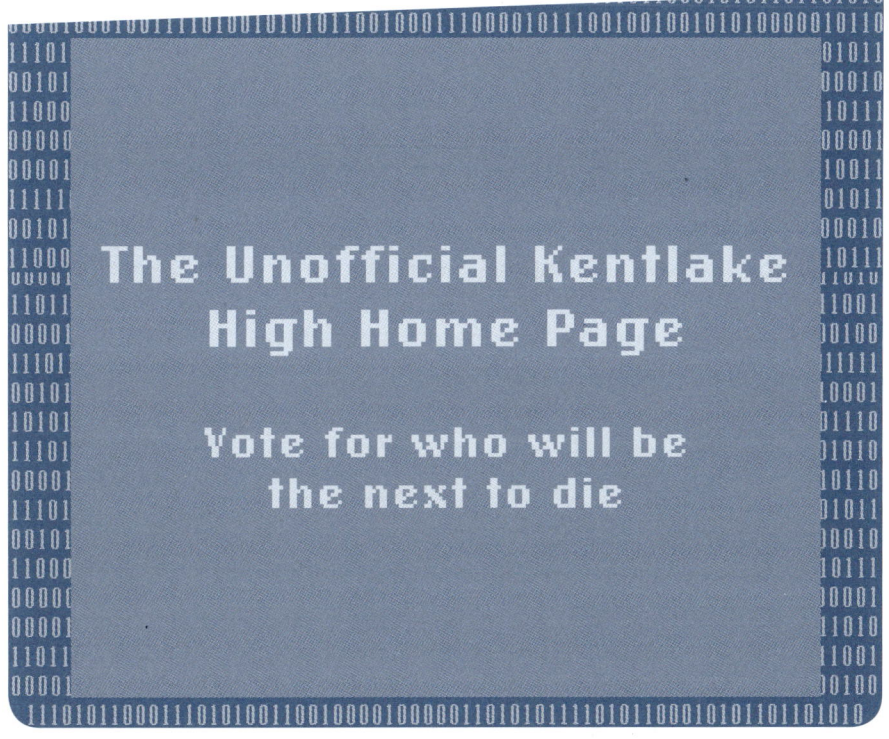

The Unofficial Kentlake High Home Page

Vote for who will be the next to die

Nick Emmett was an 18-year-old senior at Kentlake High School in Washington in 2000. He was the co-captain of the varsity basketball team and an honor student with a 3.95 GPA. He had no disciplinary record at school. As a junior, he had taken a creative writing class in which students were asked to write their own obituaries. With this in mind, Nick created "The Unofficial Kentlake High Home Page" and his father helped with the graphics. He posted mock obituaries of his friends and asked viewers to vote on who would die next—that is, who would be the subject of the next fake death notice. He included a statement that the site was for entertainment only and was not sponsored or endorsed by the school. Nick even praised some of the teachers and administrators who in turn commended Nick on his Web site. Some students asked to have their obituaries written and added to the site.

Nick never used the words "hit list" but a television news story about the site mistakenly characterized it as such. That night, Nick removed the site from the Internet. The next day the school placed him on emergency expulsion for harassment, intimidation, and disrupting the school's educational process. This was modified to a five-day suspension that included basketball practice and a play-off game.

No evidence suggested that Nick intended to intimidate or threaten anyone or that any student felt threatened by his Web site. Nick filed a complaint with the court asking for immediate relief from the school's action. He explained that he "went to court to fight for my rights because I don't think administrators should be able to make unfair punishments. I care about school and want to go to class."

HOW WOULD YOU DECIDE THIS CASE?

Do you think posting fake death notices of your friends constitutes a "hit list"? When a television reporter called it a "hit list," did it in fact become one? Why or why not? If no one felt threatened by the obituaries, should Nick have been punished for his writings? Did he cross the line of acceptable expression and create a potentially disruptive situation at school? If so, how?

WHAT THE COURT DECIDED

After considering *Tinker*, *Fraser*, and *Hazelwood* (see pages 11–14), the court found that Nick's speech was entirely beyond the school's supervision or control. The court recognized that "Web sites can be an early indication of a student's violent inclinations and can spread those beliefs quickly to like-minded or susceptible people." But in this case, Nick's writings were not intended to threaten anyone, did not pose any actual threats or manifest any violent tendencies. Nick's speech was not directed to a school assembly as in *Fraser*, nor was it in a school-sponsored format such as the *Hazelwood* newspaper. Consequently, the court ordered the school to lift the suspension, permitting Nick to return to school. The school also agreed to pay Nick nominal damages of $1.00 and his legal fees of $6,000. Nick commented that he "felt good that the judge understood my rights as a student."

HOW DOES THIS DECISION AFFECT YOU?

As you can see, even something written tongue-in-cheek can backfire. Although Nick won his case and had his school record cleared, he and his family had to put their lives on hold to deal with the school and legal issues. What began as a humorous project went seriously astray. In weighing student speech, on or off campus, both content and intent are vital in determining whether the speech is protected or not.

The bottom line: Whether you're writing a poem, essay, or screenplay, or creating a poster, diagram, or any other form of art, consider your audience and possible consequences. A good rule of thumb may be to expect the unexpected.

WHAT IS NICK DOING NOW?

Nick ended up serving one day of the suspension before the court intervened. He graduated with his class and went on to college.

RELATED CASES

Murakowski v. University of Delaware (Delaware, 2008)

Maciej Murakowski was a 19-year-old sophomore at the University of Delaware. In 2005, he created a Web site on the university's servers that included violent and sexually graphic material. He wrote fake movie reviews and satirical essays ranging from "How to Skin a Cat" to "Maciej's Official Guide to Sex." His postings were online for months before anyone complained.

When the school discovered the site, Maciej was suspended for one semester. He was prohibited from living in the residence hall until evaluated by a psychiatrist. He sued the university for violating his free speech and won in September 2008. The court called his essays "immature, crude, and highly offensive" but not a serious expression of intent to inflict harm. The judge denied his claim for actual damages but awarded him $10.00 in nominal damages.

Anthony Latour v. Riverside Beaver School District (Pennsylvania, 2005)

Anthony was a 14-year-old rapper who attended Riverside Beaver Middle School. For several years he had been writing and recording his own music at home. Some of his titles included "Murder, He Wrote," and "Massacre." His songs made reference to staff and students at his school even though he did not have a history of violence. There was no evidence that anyone felt threatened by Anthony's "battle raps" or that he communicated messages directly to anyone named in the songs. Still, the police considered his songs "terroristic threats" because they described acts of violence, and Anthony was arrested and taken from school in handcuffs. He was expelled for the following year.

Anthony sued the school district, and the court determined that no true threats were made against anyone and that the school had not been disrupted. He was allowed to return to school. A settlement was reached with the school district for $90,000, and with the police department for $60,000, for an alleged false arrest.

In the Matter of Singh (Wisconsin, 2003)

It wasn't the rap song that Sashwat Singh used when he campaigned for class treasurer that got him suspended. Instead, it was the honor student's 14-track CD that came to the attention of Brookfield High School's principal. One of the songs warned the principal that if he didn't leave the school, Singh would, "beat your ass down." The CD also contained a few sexually explicit slurs about Singh's classmates. He was suspended for five days. Since no evidence existed that he planned to act on his lyrics, the school board decided not to expel him. Sashwat did agree to see a counselor.

Imel v. Charles A. Beard School (Indiana, 2006)

"The Teddy Bear Master" was an off-campus movie made in 2006 by four Knightstown High School sophomores in Indiana. It was about an evil teddy bear that orders other stuffed animals to kill a named middle school math teacher. Apparently, the teacher had embarrassed one of the boys. The prosecutor's office reviewed the movie and declined to file any charges. However, since the 78-minute movie contained offensive language and threatened a teacher, the boys were expelled. Three of them challenged the decision in court. A settlement was reached in 2007. The expulsions were cleared from the boys' records, and they received $69,000 to split among themselves. They also wrote a letter of apology to the teacher and his wife.

THINGS TO THINK ABOUT

The Columbine High School killings of 1999 (see page 124) have focused attention on any threat of violence at school—even *hints* of violence. If you include a warning in your creative work or use such words as "unofficial" or "for entertainment only," will this protect you from being disciplined at school? Could someone still misinterpret your message and feel threatened? What is the difference between creative expression in an essay, song, or movie, and a threat to do someone harm?

Chapter 10: Further Reading and Resources

Caplan, Aaron H. "Public School Discipline for Creating Uncensored Anonymous Internet Forums." *Willamette Law Review* 39, no. 1 (Winter 2003): 93.

MacGill, Alexandra Rankin. "Parent and Teen Internet Use." PEW Internet and American Life Project, www.pewinternet.org (accessed April 11, 2014).

Markey, Justin P. "Enough Tinkering with Students' Rights: The Need for an Enhanced First Amendment Standard to Protect Off-Campus Student Internet Speech." *Capital University Law Review* 36 (Fall 2007): 129.

CHAPTER 11

When Graphic Arts Get Too Graphic

Case: *Aaron Wisniewski v. Weedsport Central School District (2007)*

Act: creating an instant message icon depicting the murder of a teacher and sending it to friends

Charge: causing immediate threat to a person, and substantially disrupting the work and discipline of the school

* Artwork based on actual icon created by Aaron Wisniewski.

In 2001, the principal of Weedsport Middle School in New York visited each class and spoke with the students about school violence. They were told that all threats would be taken seriously. Aaron was 15 and in 8th grade at Weedsport. He was present during this meeting with the principal and school social worker.

A few weeks later, Aaron created an instant message icon at home that he attached to his AOL account. The icon depicted a gun pointing to a head, a bullet leaving the gun, and blood splattering from the head. The words "Kill Mr. VanderMolen" were written under the picture. Philip VanderMolen was Aaron's English teacher. Aaron sent IM messages displaying the icon to some 15 members of his buddy list, including classmates.

The icon circulated for three weeks until Mr. VanderMolen saw it and reported it to the authorities. The police searched Aaron's backpack and locker and interviewed him and his parents. Aaron expressed regret about creating and sending the icon. He was evaluated by a psychologist who concluded that he didn't pose a threat to others and that he designed the icon as a joke. The police closed their investigation and no charges were filed.

However, the school took immediate action. Aaron was at first suspended for five days for threatening a teacher. He was also kicked off the baseball team. After hearings before the school board, Aaron was suspended for one semester. The school district arranged for tutoring during his suspension.

Aaron and his parents went to court claiming that the icon was not a true threat and therefore was protected speech. The school argued that "Kill Mr. VanderMolen" constituted threatening words that disrupted the school. Mr. VanderMolen didn't take the icon as a joke. He testified that he became anxious and fearful for his safety and for the safety of his six-month-old baby. Under the circumstances, he was not comfortable teaching Aaron, who, following his suspension, was transferred to another class for the rest of the school year.

> "THE INTERNET IS A TOY FOR SOME KIDS, JUST LIKE A CAR IS FOR SOME KIDS. THEY DON'T REALIZE HOW UTTERLY DESTRUCTIVE IT CAN BE TO TARGET SOMEONE ELSE WITH THIS TOY."
> —Professor Douglas E. Abrams, University of Missouri Law School

HOW WOULD YOU DECIDE THIS CASE?

Did the school overreact in this case? Why or why not? Is it reasonable to expect your online writings or drawings at home to be viewed by your teacher if you didn't send them to him or her? Do you think using the word "kill" made a difference in the school's response to the icon? If "kill" were left out, would the drawing itself with Mr. VanderMolen's name be enough to justify disciplinary action? Why or why not? How do you feel about the five-day suspension being extended to a full semester?

WHAT THE COURT DECIDED

The court ruled that the words "Kill Mr. Vander-Molen" and the drawing could not be viewed as anything but an immediate threat of injury to a specific person. Aaron knew the school's position on violence and that threats would be taken seriously. He created the icon anyway, sending it out to friends and classmates. Even though it was all done from home, the court said that out-of-school speech, especially threats, that could disrupt school operations, might be punished. The court's decision was in favor of the school and Aaron's lawsuit was dismissed.

The court said that "Aaron's transmission of an icon depicting and calling for the killing of his teacher . . . crosses the boundary of protected speech and constitutes student conduct that poses a foreseeable risk that the icon would come to the attention of school authorities and that it would materially and substantially disrupt the work and discipline of the school."

Aaron asked the U.S. Supreme Court to review the lower court's decision. On March 31, 2008, the Supreme Court declined to hear the case, leaving the lower court's decision in place.

HOW DOES THIS DECISION AFFECT YOU?

A single drawing or doodle could have serious consequences. If a reasonable person interprets your creation as a threat, censorship may be appropriate. Aaron probably didn't expect his icon to backfire on him. However, accompanied by a written threat to kill someone, it was no longer just a drawing. Keep in mind how others might view your work.

The bottom line: When in doubt, standard emoticons may be the way to go. When sharing your graphics or writings online, stand back from your work and ask yourself if someone else could see it differently than you do—maybe even as a threat or an act of bullying. If you have any doubt, don't send it.

> **IM and Texting Stats**
> - 68% of online teens use instant messaging.
> - The average number of text messages sent and received each month by 13- to 17-year-olds in the United States is 1,742.
> - 23% of stalking and harassment victims reported that they were harassed by some form of cell phone, texting, instant messaging, or email.

WHAT IS AARON DOING NOW?

Aaron served his suspension and returned to school the next semester. He graduated from high school and attends college, studying philosophy with an English minor. He has also tutored other students in writing. Aaron advises kids to "follow whatever passion you have no matter how insignificant or ridiculous others say it is."

RELATED CASES

In the Matter of Three Branden River High Students (Florida, 2008)

In 2008, three seniors at Branden River High School in Florida were kept from walking with their graduation class and receiving their diplomas. They had written profane rap songs that threatened to use weapons to kill school officials and sexually assault the principal's daughter. Their songs were posted on MySpace and were overheard at school on a student's iPod. The students were disciplined with work detail, suspension, and Saturday detention, in addition to being prevented from participating in graduation ceremonies. Most of the parents agreed with the school's response, with one father in tears when he saw what his son had written.

In the Matter of J.M. (Arkansas, 2000)

In a similar situation to Aaron's, although not online, 14-year-old J.M. wrote two letters to K.G., his ex-girlfriend in the summer of 2000. He threatened to stab, rape, and murder her. The letters were

> **Increase in Teacher Bullying**
> The Canadian Teachers Federation acknowledged in 2008 an increase in cyberbullying of teachers. The bullying is occurring not only on Facebook and MySpace, but also in emails and instant messages. The Federation members want the Canadian government to make cyberbullying a criminal offense. One province, Manitoba, holds cyberbullies accountable if their acts have an impact on the school, even if those acts occur outside the classroom.

written at home and weren't sent to K.G. or anyone else. However, J.M. let a friend read them, and the friend stole them the next day and gave them to K.G. She read the letters at school, became frightened, and gave them to the school resource officer. J.M. was expelled for making threats against a student. After two years in court, J.M. lost his attempt to set the expulsion aside.

Video Threats at Agawam Junior High (Massachusetts, 2008)

In September 2008, a 12-year-old boy was arrested and charged with crimes against the public and threatening to commit a crime. His name wasn't released because of his age. The 7th grader at Agawam Junior High in Massachusetts allegedly created seven "very disturbing videos" involving a knife. He made death threats against six fellow students and downloaded the videos on YouTube. He was suspended indefinitely from school and expected to undergo a psychological evaluation. He was released to his parents' custody.

> YouTube's Abuse and Safety Center allows users to block offensive comments and emails. It also provides information and reporting links regarding cyberbullying, suicide, and child exploitation. Visit www.google.com/support/youtube and explore the options by clicking "Policies, safety, and reporting."

IM Safety Tips

- What you write or draw may be copied and pasted, or forwarded to others.
- Don't talk to strangers online. Never list your last name, address, telephone number, or name of your school.
- Use a neutral screen name that won't attract predators. "Sexy," "hunk" and "hottie" are not recommended.
- Refrain from gossiping and trashtalking—it may backfire on you.
- Avoid a computer virus by using caution when clicking on links to strangers' profiles.

THINGS TO THINK ABOUT

Do you agree that art is subject to individual interpretation? Although Aaron created his icon as a joke, is it unreasonable for someone else to view it otherwise? Even if you don't send your graphic art, rap song, letter, or video directly to the person it's referencing, how do you know they won't eventually see it? Do you have control over what you post or send once it goes out—even if it's to your private friend list? The police investigate cybercrimes involving home and workplace computers all the time. Nothing exists that can't be retrieved if necessary.

Chapter 11: Further Reading and Resources

The Supreme Court • www.supremecourtus.gov
See the U.S. Supreme Court's Web site for recent decisions, oral arguments, history of the court, and current justices.

Burtka, Allison Torres. "Student's IM Threat Is Not Protected Speech." *Trial* 43 (September 2007): 68.

Hudson Jr., David L. "2nd Circuit: Schools Can Punish Students for Off-Campus Web Activity." First Amendment Center, www.firstamendmentcenter.org (accessed April 11, 2014).

Hudson Jr., David L. "Silencing Student Speech—and Even Artwork—in the Post-Columbine Era: The Relevant Supreme Court Cases, and How They Have Been Misapplied." FindLaw, writ.lp.findlaw.com/commentary/20040304_jr..html (accessed April 11, 2014).

CHAPTER 12

Prank or Plan?

Case: *State v. Joshua Mortimer (2001)*

Act: posting an ominous screensaver message on a school computer

Charge: communicating a threat

On April 20, 1999, Dylan Klebold and Eric Harris went on a shooting rampage at Columbine High School in Colorado. They killed 12 fellow students, a teacher, and finally themselves. Eric had a Web site that contained numerous rants about violence, including the phrase, "God, I can't wait until I can kill you people." For a school project, Harris and Klebold made a video titled "Hitman for Hire." After the tragedy, school officials, students, and parents across the nation were afraid that copycat crimes would occur in their own schools.

Hoggard High School in North Carolina was no exception. Within days of Columbine, rumors began to circulate throughout the student body that Hoggard High was to be bombed on May 4, 1999. Parents were asked to come to the school that day and patrol the halls to help the students feel safe. One-fifth of the students were absent on May 4.

That day a student at school discovered a screensaver message that read, "The end is near." The police traced the message to 17-year-old Joshua Mortimer, a Hoggard sophomore. He was arrested at school and spent two weeks in jail before his parents could raise the thousands of dollars for his bail. Josh admitted to writing the message on the school's computer. He said he didn't mean anything by it other than "the end of the school year or the end of time, or whatever." He said it was a joke referring to the year 2000 being the end of the world. Josh was charged with communicating a threat and was tried as an adult. He was found guilty by a jury and sentenced to 45 days in jail, 18 months probation, and 48 hours of community service. Josh was also expelled from school for one year.

Josh appealed the jury's decision claiming the state failed to prove that he committed a crime. At the time of this incident, communicating a threat was a misdemeanor in North Carolina. The misdemeanor had four elements that must be proven by the state: (1) a person willfully threatens to physically injure someone or damage someone's property; (2) the threat is communicated to the other person; (3) the threat is made in such a way that a reasonable person would believe that it is likely to be carried out; and (4) the person threatened believes that the threat will be carried out. Without proof of these four elements, a conviction for communicating a threat cannot stand. The state argued to the jury that Josh's crime contained all four elements.

HOW WOULD YOU DECIDE THIS CASE?

Do you think Josh's note contained all the state's required elements of communicating a threat? Why or why not? Did Josh threaten anyone in particular by posting "The end is near" on the school's computer? Would you interpret "The end is near" as a message directed at you personally? Under the circumstances, was the school justified in calling in the police to investigate what may have been a prank? Do you think this would have been handled differently if there had been no prior rumor of a bomb on the same day? Or if Josh had posted his message before Columbine occurred? Why or why not?

WHAT THE COURT DECIDED

The court started its analysis of the case by stating: "The meaning of the statement 'The end is near' is impossible to ascertain. The end of what is near? Who will bring about the 'end' and how?" The court recognized that the school was in a state of fear over the tragedy of Columbine and that one interpretation of Josh's message was that the writer intended to bomb the school. The court ruled, however, that, "the leap to such a conclusion beyond a reasonable doubt is extremely speculative."

Before this incident, Josh had no problems at school and even the police officer who arrested Josh thought his message was a prank. No evidence was found that he had any plan to injure anyone or damage school property. He wasn't connected to any of the alleged bomb threats at the school. Since the statement "The end is near" did not indicate what, if anything, the speaker intended to do, the court threw out the jury's verdict and dismissed the charge against Josh.

HOW DOES THIS DECISION AFFECT YOU?

Four words typed into a screensaver changed Josh's life. It was over two years before he won his appeal to the North Carolina Court of Appeals. In the meantime, he couldn't return to his high school, he spent two weeks in jail, and he had to complete his probation term and the community service hours. The court suspended the 45-day jail sentence, which meant he didn't have to spend any more time in jail.

Admittedly, Josh's timing couldn't have been worse. Following Columbine, the country was on a high alert for school violence. Hundreds of bomb threats were phoned in to the nation's schools. At any other time, "The end is near" might have been taken lightly or even ignored.

The bottom line: Think before you act. As Josh learned, there may be a stiff price for not considering unintended consequences.

> "FEAR OF SERIOUS INJURY CANNOT ALONE JUSTIFY SUPPRESSION OF FREE SPEECH AND ASSEMBLY. MEN FEARED WITCHES AND BURNT WOMEN. IT IS THE FUNCTION OF SPEECH TO FREE MEN FROM THE BONDAGE OF IRRATIONAL FEARS."
> —from *Whitney v. California*, 1927
>
> "UNDIFFERENTIATED FEAR OR APPREHENSION OF DISTURBANCE IS NOT ENOUGH TO OVERCOME THE RIGHT TO FREEDOM OF EXPRESSION."
> —from *Tinker v. Des Moines Independent Community School District*, 1969

WHAT IS JOSH DOING NOW?

After being expelled, Josh earned a GED at a local community college. He works in the pizza industry, is married, and has a young son. Josh advises kids to "be extremely careful about what you say, do, and write while in school."

RELATED CASES

Dustin Mitchell v. Rolla Public Schools (Missouri, 1999)

Dustin was a junior at Rolla High School in Missouri in 1999. He was an 18-year-old honor student eligible for the National Honor Society. Five days after the killings at Columbine High School, Dustin participated in an online chat room about school violence. He was at home, and in response to the question, "Do you think such a tragedy could happen at your school?" he answered, "Yes!"

Dustin used another student's name instead of his own—a student who regularly wore a black trench coat to school, similar to those worn by the shooters at Columbine. Dustin was quickly identified as the writer and was suspended for 10 days. He was also given 40 hours of community service to complete at the police department.

Dustin took the matter to court and won. The court ruled that his speech was protected and that the school's code of conduct wasn't clear about off-campus speech.

State v. Brittini Hardcastle and four others (Florida, 2008)

As was shown in Josh's case, you don't have to be an adult to be treated like one in the criminal justice system. Every state has laws about trying minors in adult court for certain crimes. Conviction results in adult sentences, including life in prison. The decision to prosecute you as a minor or as an adult depends in part on your state's laws, your age, your criminal history, and the current offense. Consider the following recent case of juveniles being prosecuted as adults.

Victoria Lindsay was a 16-year-old cheerleader and honor student at Mulberry High School in Florida. During spring break in 2008, she was staying at the home of her friend, Mercades. Brittini, Mercades, and three other girls, ages 14 to 18, confronted Victoria about trash-talking them on MySpace. One of the girls also sent threatening text messages to Victoria the same day. Later they assaulted her for 30 minutes while one of the girls videotaped the beating and posted it on YouTube and MySpace—a form of

> **Tragedy at Red Lake**
> In 2005, 16-year-old Jeffrey James Weiss shot and killed his grandfather and his grandfather's girlfriend at home. He then went to school and killed five students, a teacher, and an unarmed security guard before taking his own life in a classroom at Red Lake High School in Minnesota. Prior to the killings, Jeffrey left numerous postings on the Internet about his thoughts and the hardships of his life that led to his depression and "a darker path than most choose to take."

cyberbulling known as "happy slapping." During the assault, Victoria was hit in the face and her head was slammed into a wall. She lost consciousness and when she awoke, the beating continued. She tried to leave but the girls kept her there until she was driven to another location and released. She was threatened with another beating if she reported what happened.

> **Happy slapping** is an extreme form of bullying where physical assaults are recorded on cell phones or other devices and posted on the Internet.

All of the teens involved were arrested and taken to jail. They were charged as adults with felony kidnapping, which carries a maximum sentence of life imprisonment, and felony battery with a maximum of one year in jail. In 2009, all of the girls entered guilty pleas to lesser charges in exchange for dismissal of the kidnapping charge. They were sentenced to probation, restitution to Victoria and a letter of apology, and community service hours. They were also ordered not to have contact with Victoria or the media while on probation, and not to use social networking sites. Brittini, a key figure in the beating, was sentenced to jail for 15 days.

In the Matter of Seven Girls (Indiana, 2008)

Two weeks after Victoria's beating, an apparent copycat instance of happy slapping occurred in Indiana. Seven girls ages 12 to 14 lured a 12-year-old classmate to a parking lot. All of the girls went to Clarksville Middle School. An argument escalated into a fight where the victim, the daughter of a police officer, was hit with rocks and fists resulting in head trauma and a chipped tooth. The fight was videotaped by one of the assailants and posted on PhotoBucket. The girls were charged with battery and disorderly conduct. Since the incident happened off-campus, the school took no action against them.

THINGS TO THINK ABOUT

Although Josh's screensaver message was presumably a prank with no malicious intent, his age and timing worked against him. Before trying a juvenile as an adult, what factors should the court take into consideration? Does a juvenile's family life matter? What about his or her school disciplinary record? Should the teen's potential for rehabilitation be a factor? Are some crimes so outrageous that adult punishment should be a given, no matter what the defendant's age? If so, where would you draw the line? And if not, why?

> "THE POLICY OF THE JUVENILE LAW WAS TO HIDE YOUTHFUL ERRORS FROM FULL GAZE OF THE PUBLIC AND BURY THEM IN THE GRAVEYARD OF FORGOTTEN PAST."
> —*Arizona v. Guerrero*, 1942

Chapter 12: Further Reading and Resources

Harpaz, Leora. "Internet Speech and First Amendment Rights of Public School Students." *Brigham Young University Law Review* (2000): 123.

Hudson Jr., David L. "Censorship of Student Internet Speech: The Effect of Diminishing Student Rights, Fear of the Internet and Columbine." *Detroit College of Law at Michigan State University Law Review* (2000): 199.

Salgado, Richard. "Protecting Student Speech Rights While Increasing School Safety: School Jurisdiction and the Search for Warning Signs in a Post-Columbine/Red Lake Environment." *Brigham Young University Law Review*, no. 5 (2005): 1371–1412.

CHAPTER 13

Know Thy Student Handbook

Case: *Jack Flaherty Jr. v. Keystone Oaks School District* (2003)

Act: posting critical messages on a school sports team's electronic message board

Charge: bringing disrespect and adverse attention to the school and its programs

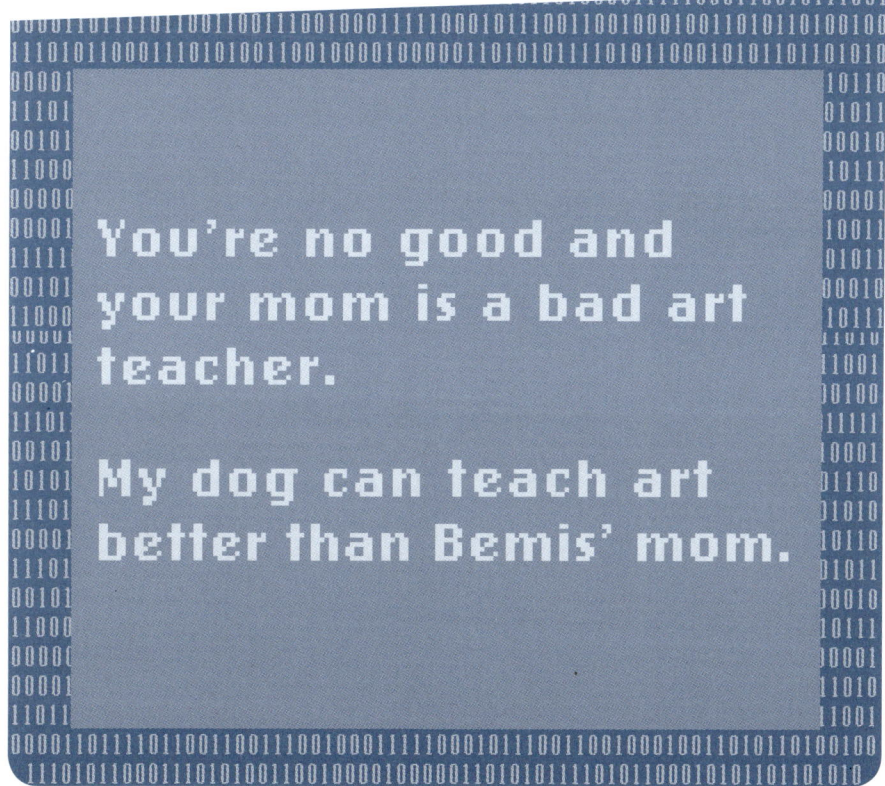

Pat Bemis was a student at Baldwin High School in Pennsylvania and on the varsity volleyball team. Baldwin's rivals attended Keystone Oaks High School in 2001. The statements on page 131 were posted on a volleyball message board by senior Jack Flaherty Jr., a member of Keystone's volleyball team. Pat's mother was an art teacher at Keystone Oaks. The statements were part of a series of messages Jack posted about a game between the rival teams. Three of the messages were posted from home, and one from a school computer with permission from his teacher. None of the messages contained any profanity or threats. They included typical bragging rights such as, "Someone better call the Guinness Book of World Records for the biggest lashing in men's volleyball history."

Keystone Oaks had a student handbook that included discipline, student responsibility, and technology provisions. After the school learned of Jack's messages, he was kicked off the volleyball team, prohibited from participating in after-school events, and forbidden to use any school computers.

Jack and his parents sued the school district claiming a violation of Jack's free speech. They also said the student handbook was so vague that students could be muzzled for expressing their opinions. In standing up for the right of students to use the Internet from home, Jack said he was fighting the case "because I knew kids were getting punished for reasons the school couldn't justify." The school believed it could discipline a student for bringing negative attention to the school and to the volleyball team.

HOW WOULD YOU DECIDE THIS CASE?

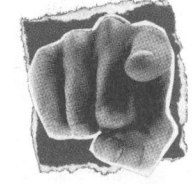

Are you surprised at the school's response to Jack's online comments? Or did his taunts go too far? Why or why not? Would the situation be any different if all postings by Jack were made on a school computer rather than his own? His only comment from a school computer was, "How bad is Keystone Oaks going to beat Baldwin? I predict a lashing and for Bemis to shed tears." Do you think this justified action by the school? Why or why not?

WHAT THE COURT DECIDED

Before Jack's case was scheduled for trial, he settled with the school district for $60,000 (for attorney fees and damages). The only issue remaining for the court to decide was whether the Keystone Student Handbook was unconstitutionally vague.

A rule or law that is considered overbroad or vague is one that punishes both protected and unprotected speech. For example, the student handbook at Keystone prohibited speech that was "inappropriate, harassing, offensive, or abusive." No further definition of these terms was provided. The court found that the handbook policies "do not provide the students with adequate warning" of the conduct that is prohibited.

The principal of the school believed he could discipline a student for bringing disrespect and adverse attention to the school and its programs. But under the *Tinker* test (see pages 11–12), Jack's comments did not rise to the level of substantial disruption at school. "The mere desire to avoid 'discomfort' or 'unpleasantness' is not enough to justify restricting student speech."

The court went further and considered whether the school could discipline a student for off-campus activities. The principal and athletic coach testified that they could, if the expression affected the school negatively or brought shame to the school or its programs. The court disagreed, arguing that the student handbook was unconstitutionally vague since it "could be read to cover speech that occurs off the school's campus and is not school related."

Jack later said that he hoped "in the future Keystone Oaks will not punish students who exercise their constitutional rights to criticize the school."

HOW DOES THIS DECISION AFFECT YOU?

The court's ruling affirms your right to criticize, applaud, spoof, or comment about teachers, staff, classmates, and rivals. If the school has rules of conduct regarding use of its computers, they must be clear and unambiguous. Any prohibited behavior must be spelled out in the student handbook for all to see. Jack's Web writings were no different from making the same comments in the hallway, on the volleyball court, or in the locker room. They may have been offensive, but they constituted protected speech.

The bottom line: Your speech may be protected, but think twice before criticizing someone's mother—that's always a hot button!

WHAT IS JACK DOING NOW?

Jack graduated from Keystone Oaks High School and went on to attend Indiana University of Pennsylvania.

RELATED CASES

In the Matter of Tony Harris (Michigan, 2009)

Tony Harris was a 19-year-old sophomore at Calvin College in Michigan. After breaking up with his girlfriend, he posted sexual comments about her on Facebook. He was already on school probation for a similar incident. In February 2009, he was expelled from the college for violating the school's technology and conduct code. Tony maintained that the girl used his password to post the comment herself.

Message Boards at Work

Jack's case involved school online message boards, while a developing area of the law involves message boards at the workplace. They are popping up at businesses around the country, allowing employees to post comments to anyone in the company. Liability issues for employers include sexual harassment in the workplace, discrimination, defamation, and claims of wrongful discipline or firing.

In 2008, two California college students, Sarah Doolittle and Austin Garrido, were campus representatives for Uloop, an online marketplace for students.

Thomas Siefert v. Lancaster High School (Ohio, 2003)

Thomas Siefert was a 17-year-old junior at Lancaster High School in Ohio. In 2003, he created the Web site www.lancasternewsletter.com where he included pictures of teachers and a message board with negative comments about the school and administrators. Although parts of the site were crude and tasteless, Thomas did all of the work away from school. The site was up for almost a year before he shut it down to avoid getting into trouble. The school suspended Thomas for 10 days and later voted to expel him for the remainder of the school year. Following a meeting with the school board, the expulsion was lifted and Thomas was allowed to return to school and make up the work he missed.

> "WHAT THE INTERNET GIVES IS THE ILLUSION OF PRIVACY, BUT IN FACT, IT'S THE EXACT OPPOSITE. THERE IS LESS ANONYMITY AND PRIVACY THAN EVER. EVENTUALLY, EVERYTHING THAT GETS WRITTEN AND COMMUNICATED CAN BE TRACED TO ITS ORIGINATOR."
> —Professor Thierry Guedj, Boston University

Kim v. Newport High School (Washington, 1995)

In 1995, Paul Kim was weeks away from graduating from Newport High School in Washington. He had applied to Columbia, Harvard, and Stanford Universities. At home he created the "Unofficial Newport High School Home Page" where he made fun of his classmates for majoring in football and being preoccupied with sex. He

---

They discussed forming a union on their company's message board. Within an hour the postings were removed and the students were fired. They filed a complaint with the National Labor Relations Board, which oversees employment problems. At issue was whether the subject discussed and the speech itself was a protected activity at work. This was one of the first cases regarding email and message board communications in the workplace. The Board ruled in favor of the students and a settlement was reached that included back pay. Austin and Sarah chose not to return to work at Uloop.

added links to *Playboy*'s Web site and submitted the site to Yahoo for listing.

After complaints to the school about content, Paul removed the site from Yahoo and deactivated the home page altogether. The principal withdrew her recommendation for college admission and her endorsement of Paul as a National Merit Scholarship finalist, which carried a $2,000 award. Paul sued the school district for violating his right to free expression. The case was settled when the school apologized to Paul, reimbursed him for the $2,000 scholarship award, and had him reinstated as a National Merit Scholar. Paul was later accepted at Columbia University.

THINGS TO THINK ABOUT

At the beginning of the school year, does your school require you and your parents to sign a statement that you've received the student handbook? Have you read through it and become familiar with the rules? Do any of the rules seem vague or overly broad? If so, which ones and why? Does your school have an Acceptable Use Policy (AUP) regarding the school's computers? Does the policy also apply to on-campus access of a personal computer? The code of conduct probably doesn't spell out every activity that may be questionable at school, especially in this age of ever-changing technology. But does it have to? What about common sense? (See chapter 8 for more on this topic.)

> In 2008, eight students at a Virginia high school were suspended for 10 days for violating the school's Acceptable Use Policy. Afterward they were hired by the school to find the weak spots in the school district's network.

Chapter 13: Further Reading and Resources

Adamovich, Tracy L. "Return to Sender: Off-Campus Speech Brought On-Campus by Another Student." *St. John's Law Review* 82 (Summer 2008): 1087.

Cassel, Christi. "Keep Out of MySpace! Protecting Students from Unconstitutional Suspensions and Expulsions." *William and Mary Law Review* 49 (November 2007): 643.

Freeman, Simone Marie. "Upholding Students' Due Process Rights: Why Students Are in Need of Better Representation at, and Alternatives to, School Suspension Hearings." *Family Court Review* 45 (October 2007): 638.

Strossen, Nadine. "Keeping the Constitution Inside the Schoolhouse Gates: Students Thirty Years After *Tinker v. Des Moines Independent Community School District.*" *Drake University Law Review* 48 (2000): 445.

Zirkel, Perry A. "The Supreme Court Speaks on Student Expression: A Revised Map." *West's Education Law Reporter* 221 (September 2007): 485.

CHAPTER 14

Are You Responsible for Everything on Your Site?

Case: *Ryan Dwyer v. Oceanport School District* (2005)

Act: creating a Web page that contained negative comments posted by other students

Charge: publishing online content that caused disruption at school and included threats to others' safety

This was Ryan Dwyer's greeting on the Web page he created at home in 2003. Ryan was 14 and in 8th grade at Maple Place School in New Jersey. His site included an About page, Favorite Links, and a Guestbook. His About page contained his own comments about school, such as:

- It's fun to disrupt class, especially in Mrs. Hirshfield's room!
- Start protests, they aren't illegal.
- MAPLE PLACE IS THE WORST SCHOOL ON THE PLANET!
- Wear political T-shirts to annoy the teachers.
- Use your First Amendment right wisely.
- THIS PAGE PROTECTED BY THE U.S. CONSTITUTION.

Ryan's Favorite Links contained links to music groups, body piercing sites, and sites devoted to the constitutional rights of public school students. His Guestbook invited visitors to post their own messages and comments. Ryan warned guests against profanity and threats:

"Please sign my guestbook but NO PROFANITY AT ALL!!!!!!! and no threats to any teacher or person EVER. If you think it may be a bad word or it may be threatening DO NOT TYPE IT IN."

Ryan later stated that he created the site because he felt he had no voice at school. "You need your First Amendment rights to get change," he later stated at a news conference.

Due to the applications he used, Ryan had no control over messages posted on his site. He wasn't able to edit any posts and could only delete the entire Guestbook. Several visitors used profanity and ethnic slurs, and others made threats against the school and the principal. "The principal is a fat piece of crap," one declared. "He should walk his fat ass into oncoming traffic."

The principal saw the site and called the police. Ryan was suspended for five days and removed from the baseball team for one month. He was also excluded from a class trip to Philadelphia. He and his parents challenged the discipline imposed and asked the district court to intervene.

HOW WOULD YOU DECIDE THIS CASE?

Based on what you've read about Ryan's Web site, was the school correct in disciplining him? Should Ryan be free from any responsibility for his site because he posted a warning? Should you be responsible for the postings of others on your Web pages? Why or why not? Was Ryan inciting disruption at school by encouraging students to annoy teachers? What do you think of his reference to the U.S. Constitution and student rights?

WHAT THE COURT DECIDED

In 1996, Congress passed The Communications Decency Act, which applies to this case. In part, it states that anyone who creates a Web site is not responsible for information added to it by other sources. In other words, you can't punish someone for the conduct and words of another person. This means that the visitors to Ryan's Guestbook became content providers and were held accountable for their own comments. Under the law, Ryan was not responsible for their postings.

If Ryan's own comments on his Web site constituted a true threat, they were unprotected speech. The school could punish him without violating his free speech rights. The court stated that "in light of the violence prevalent in schools today, school officials are justified in taking very seriously student threats against faculty or other students." In Ryan's case, however, there was no evidence that the material that Ryan posted on his site was intended to threaten anyone or manifest any violent tendencies. The comments made by others in his Guestbook are not attributable to Ryan.

Did Ryan's Web site disrupt the school? If it did, he could be disciplined. But the disruption had to be more than the discomfort or unpleasantness that accompanies an unpopular viewpoint, as previous cases ruled. The mere fact that content causes hurt feelings or resentment does not render the expression unprotected. The court found no disruption caused by Ryan's online expression.

Although ruling in Ryan's favor, the court did not decide the issue of money damages against the principal and school superintendent. Those issues were left for a jury to decide. However, an agreement was reached and the school district agreed to pay Ryan $117,500 for damages and attorney fees.

Following the settlement, Ryan said, "While my parents and I are happy the case is resolved, most importantly, I'm hopeful this will help ensure that free speech rights of students aren't trampled on again."

> "IT IS IMPERATIVE TO DISTINGUISH BETWEEN THE CONTENT POSTED BY RYAN HIMSELF AND THE COMMENTS POSTED BY VISITORS TO HIS WEB SITE . . . BECAUSE RYAN DID NOT HIMSELF PUBLISH ANY MATERIAL WHICH CAUSED A DISRUPTION OF THE SCHOOL, HE COULD NOT BE DISCIPLINED WITHOUT VIOLATING HIS FIRST AMENDMENT RIGHT TO FREE SPEECH."
> —from Ryan Dwyer's case decision

How Does This Decision Affect You?

This case covers an issue not addressed by other cases. When you create a Web page, you have the option of inviting others to comment on it. You can limit this to approved friends, or you can open it up to the world. Either way, you have no control over what others will say. Ryan tried to keep it clean by including a direct warning.

The bottom line: Depending on the applications you are using, you may not be able to control what others post on your Web page. It's advisable to add a warning to posters and monitor your page closely. Keep in mind, however, that even if you include a warning, people may post material on your site that could possibly lead to school disruption or other charges.

WHAT IS RYAN DOING NOW?

Ryan graduated from high school and attends William and Mary College in Virginia.

RELATED CASES

Larson v. Birdville High School (Texas, 2005)

Kelsey Larson was a freshman cheerleader at Birdville High School in Texas. In 2005, one of her friends posted a derogatory statement about other cheerleaders on Kelsey's Xanga blog. School officials claimed it violated the code of conduct for cheerleaders and Kelsey was kicked off the team. She and her parents fought the discipline and won. Kelsey returned to the team the next semester.

Goldsmith and Morgan v. Brookwood High School (Georgia, 2003)

Lloyd Goldsmith Jr. and Edward Morgan were senior honor students at Brookwood High School in Georgia. In 2003, they commented about one of their teachers on another student's Web site. Lloyd described a fictional assault on the teacher and wrote, "Filthy whore's gotta die!" Edward added that he wanted to impale the teacher with a fence post. He later retracted the comment saying it was meant as a joke. Both students were suspended and ordered to complete community service hours. The boys and their parents sued the school district asking that all disciplinary action be removed from their records. The case was settled out-of-court with the district agreeing to clear the students' records and pay each $95,000.

Curzon-Brown v. Lathouwer (California, 2000)

Ryan Lathouwer had a frustrating semester at San Francisco City College. Tired of the unpredictable quality of teachers and classes, he started a private Web site called "Teacher Review." The site allowed students to post evaluations of their teachers using an A through F scale. Users could also post comments anonymously. Ryan did not edit posted reviews, giving students free reign of the site. In less than a year, the site had nearly 18,000 hits. Ryan commented, "Most of the reviews are positive—the derogatory ones are students' opinions and they have a right to voice their opinions, even if it's not in the most intelligent way." When brought to his attention, Ryan removed offensive material from the site.

English professor Daniel Curzon-Brown was angered by reviews that rated him as one of the 10 worst teachers at the college. His ratings also included profane language and attacked his sexual orientation. He sued Ryan and the college for defamation and sought an order preventing future defamatory reviews. Just before trial, the professor agreed to dismiss his lawsuit and pay part of Ryan's legal fees. It became apparent to him that he did not have a winning case. The settlement was considered a major victory for free speech on the Internet, and for student media everywhere.

THINGS TO THINK ABOUT

If you have your own Web site, profile page, or blog, do you have control over the comments or postings others add to it? Does your page include a disclaimer or warning about profanity or offensive comments? If you can edit comments before posting them, how do you decide what's ethical or decent? If you question whether someone's comment is appropriate, is it sometimes better to leave it out all together? These are some questions to ask yourself as you sign on to social networking sites and participate in online discussions.

Chapter 14: Further Reading and Resources

iSafe • xblock.isafe.org
This nonprofit organization, endorsed by Congress, can help you promote online safety. Become an iMentor and download your very own Student Toolkit to share information with friends and family.

Weng, Garner K. "Type No Evil: The Proper Latitude of Public Educational Institutions in Restricting Expressions of Their Students on the Internet." *Hastings Communication and Entertainment Law Journal* 20 (1998): 751.

Wenkart, Ronald D. "Discipline of K–12 Students for Conduct Off School Grounds." *West's Education Law Reporter* 210 (August 2006): 531.

CHAPTER 15

So You Want to Be a Hacker?

Case: *Justin Boucher v. School District of Greenfield (1998)*

Act: published instructions in a student newspaper for hacking into a school's computer system

Charge: endangerment of school property

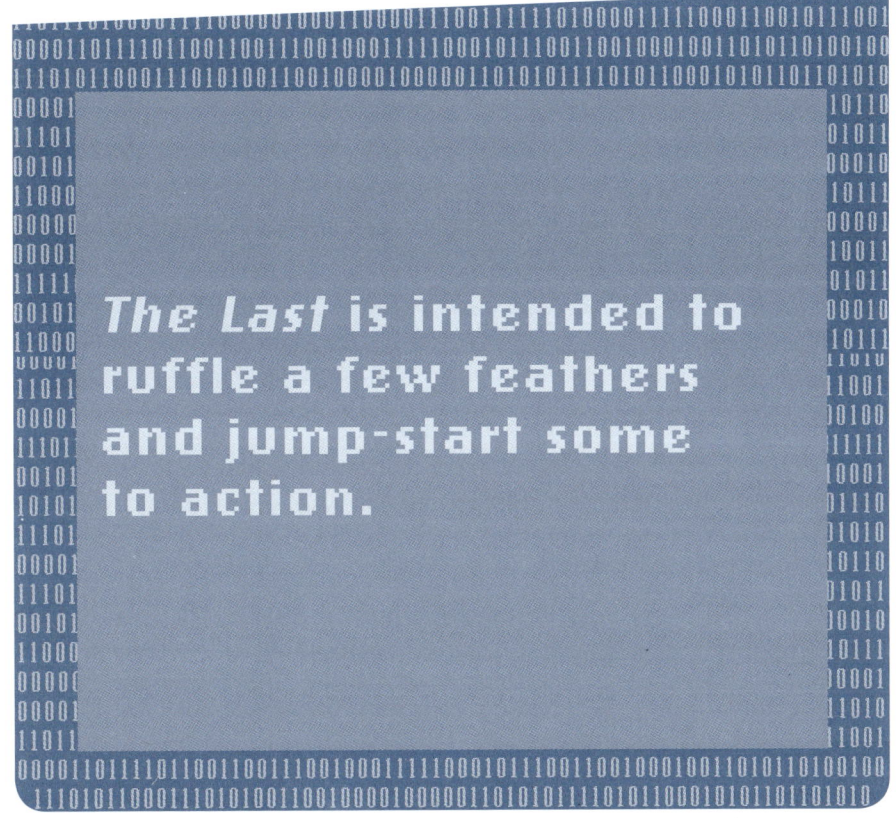

The Last is intended to ruffle a few feathers and jump-start some to action.

This was the stated purpose of underground newspaper *The Last* in its April 1997 inaugural issue. In the June issue, 17-year-old junior Justin Boucher wrote an article titled "So You Want to Be a Hacker." Justin was a junior at Greenfield High School in Wisconsin when he distributed 500 copies of the paper on campus. The article aimed to instruct everyone how to hack into the school's computers. It was written under the byline "Sacco and Vanzetti," which was quickly traced to Justin. He used this name because he claimed, "Every time something went wrong with the computers, I was blamed."

The article began with a statement about some students being blamed for a computer virus at school. Justin wrote that the incompetence of the school's computer experts was the problem. He explained that since their parents' tax dollars paid for the school's computers, students had a right to know what was on them. Justin created a list of hacker's ethics encouraging hacking activities but advising against harming any person or property.

> **The Real Sacco and Vanzetti**
> Nicola Sacco, 28, and Bartolomeo Vanzetti, 31, were immigrant anarchists convicted of murder and armed robbery in 1920 in Massachusetts. They received the death penalty and were executed by electrocution on August 23, 1927. Their case was controversial, with many believing they were innocent.

Justin provided specific instructions for how to enter the school's computer system. The hacker would then have access to the login names of all the students and teachers. He also wrote that if a hacker saw that a teacher was online at the time, "then I would suggest not doing any hacking because you might get caught." He included a disclaimer advising anyone who got into trouble to "Just say 'God made me do it' and they might let you off." Justin ended the article with a threat against anyone who took credit for his work or claimed to be "Sacco and Vanzetti."

Two weeks before the school year ended, Justin was suspended and later expelled for one year. He was told the expulsion was because the article had endangered school property. Even though

Justin wrote the article away from school, he distributed it at school and gave unauthorized persons access to school information and programs. His article constituted a crime under Wisconsin law. However, no criminal charges were filed.

Justin asked the district court to immediately lift the expulsion since it would keep him from graduating with his class. He claimed that the article was mere advocacy and that his motive was to increase computer literacy among the students. He argued that he had a right to speak out "whether in the cafeteria, or on the playing field, or on the campus," quoting *Tinker* (see pages 11–12). Since he didn't use a school computer, he argued that expulsion was unjustified.

The school supported the expulsion by claiming that an unauthorized person could alter students' grades and disciplinary information entered by teachers. According to the school, Justin violated its computer policies even if the article was not a criminal act. They offered Justin an alternative study program so he could graduate the following year with his class.

HOW WOULD YOU DECIDE THIS CASE?

Are you free to write anything you like away from school? Or does the effect of your writings come into play? Do you think Justin's case would have been different if he hadn't handed out his newspaper at school? What if *The Last* was never distributed on campus, but was seen by a teacher months later—do you think Justin would still be in trouble? Does the fact that he advocated on-campus activity (hacking into the school's computers) make any difference? Do you think a year expulsion was too severe of a consequence? Why or why not?

WHAT THE COURT DECIDED

"*The Last* is not your father's newspaper." This was the first sentence in the court's decision about Justin's case. The court weighed the harm to Justin if the one-year expulsion remained against the harm to the school if they granted his request to lift the expulsion. They concluded that

Justin was a self-proclaimed hacker whose article created a serious threat to school property. They stated that if the expulsion was set aside, allowing Justin to return to school, that "school discipline, undertaken reasonably and in good faith to protect the school's vital interests," would be undermined.

Witnesses testified that computer experts spent hours conducting diagnostic tests for signs of tampering. All of the school's passwords mentioned in Justin's article were changed. However, the potential for future disruption existed, especially in view of Justin's offer to "teach you more" once the reader mastered this first lesson. The court considered the article to be a blueprint for invading the school's computer system, with encouragement to do just that, and rejected Justin's claim that the school had to show actual harm. The expulsion remained in effect.

> "WITHOUT FIRST ESTABLISHING DISCIPLINE AND MAINTAINING ORDER, TEACHERS CANNOT BEGIN TO EDUCATE THEIR STUDENTS."
>
> "THE SCHOOLROOM IS THE FIRST OPPORTUNITY MOST CITIZENS HAVE TO EXPERIENCE THE POWER OF GOVERNMENT— THE VALUES THEY LEARN THERE, THEY TAKE WITH THEM IN LIFE."
>
> —both quotes from *New Jersey v. T.L.O.* (1985)

HOW DOES THIS DECISION AFFECT YOU?

Some students have turned to writing their own articles and stories, rather than writing for the school newspaper or yearbook. This allows them to be more creative and cover controversial subjects. They have a legal right to author and distribute such publications as long as they don't create a substantial disruption at school—back to the *Tinker* test.

Hacking may be used as a form of cyberbullying, even if it does not involve a direct personal attack on someone. In this case, the school was the target. When a hacker breaks into someone's email or bank account, victims suffer injuries including financial loss and invasion of privacy.

> *The bottom line:* Recognize and respect the rights of others, even in cyberspace. Being labeled a hacker is nothing to be proud of, unless you're a "white hat hacker" and use your skills for good instead of evil. (See next page.)

WHAT IS JUSTIN DOING NOW?

Justin decided not to fight the case any longer. He accepted the court's decision and the school's offer to study at home so he could graduate on schedule. Justin is now a professional poker dealer and player in Las Vegas and operates an eBay business dealing with the online version of the card game, *Magic: The Gathering*.

NOT ALL HACKERS ARE EQUAL

The word "hacker" gets a bad rap. As you'll read in the following stories, there are good and bad hackers. Those who do it for personal financial gain or notoriety are known as "black hat hackers." "White hat hackers" work for private industry or the government. Their job is to stay one step ahead of the black hats and improve computer and security systems. Even schools have used students to help secure computer systems against attack by the bad guys.

> **Black Hat Hackers**
> In February 2008, 18-year-old Jonah Greenthal was a senior at New Trier High School in Illinois. He wanted to know his class ranking. He was caught on campus using his laptop to break into the school's network. He was charged with computer tampering and faced a year in jail and a $1,000 fine. He was also suspended from school, missed his senior prom, and couldn't walk with his graduating class.
>
> In 2003, an 11-year-old student at Saint Lucie Middle School in Florida told his teacher that he needed to return to the classroom to get his lunch. While there, he got on his teacher's computer and changed his grades. He was arrested and charged with a felony for altering data in the computer. He was later released to his father and suspended for 10 days. The charges were dropped after he successfully completed a diversion program through the juvenile court and wrote a letter of apology.

White Hat Hackers

Anzar High School in California required students to complete projects in math, science, language arts, and history before graduating. For one of his projects, student Reid Ellison was given permission to hack into the school's computer grading system. He did so in a matter of seconds and, ironically, *lowered* his 4.0 GPA to a 1.9. Reid got an A on his project, and used his hacking skills to help the school improve its security system.

In July 2008, 18-year-old Owen Thor Walker admitted to hacking into the computer system at the University of Pennsylvania. He was facing five years in prison when he agreed to an $11,000 fine and to work with the police as a white hat hacker to solve computer crimes in exchange for a clean record.

The U.S. federal government seeks out ethical hackers to analyze threats to the nation's computer systems. In an effort to protect information networks against an attack, the Pentagon plans to train 250 cyber experts by 2011. The Homeland Security Department placed a want ad in 2009 for a white hat hacker who could "think like the bad guy." The government is also looking for 10,000 high school and college students to work as cyber-warriors and cyber-guardians. A talent search is underway. Visit www.uscyberchallenge.org for details.

Cyber-Cheating

In a 2008 survey, 64% of U.S. high school students said they cheated on a test. And now, the age-old problem of cheating has entered the digital era. Technology and the Internet have opened a world of possibilities and temptations, including video cheating tutorials on YouTube, camera phones with answer sheets, text messages from friends outside the classroom, plagiarizing assignments, and hacking into school computer systems to alter grades.

"TrainReq" was an appropriate screen name for 19-year-old Josh Holly of Tennessee. In 2008, he hacked into the email account of Disney star Miley Cyrus (Hannah Montana). He stole sexually explicit photos of her and posted them online. Josh bragged about his antics in blogs, claiming he'd never get caught. In October 2008, the FBI searched his home and removed three computers and his cell phone. The FBI continues to gather evidence and charges may be filed.

RELATED CASES

State v. Schick (Minnesota, 2007)

In October 2007, at Atwater High School in Minnesota, 17-year-old Cozy Lynn Schick hacked into another teenager's MySpace account. Cozy then sent messages to friends listed in the account saying she planned to bring a gun to school to "kill everyone." The school was locked down and the police were called. With the help of MySpace employees, the messages were traced to Cozy and she was arrested and charged with making terrorist threats. She pleaded

Josh is also suspected of hacking into the MySpace accounts of celebrities Rihanna, Chris Brown, Linkin Park, and Fall Out Boy.

"Mafiaboy" was the nickname used by a 15-year-old Canadian high school student. He jammed major Web sites including CNN, Amazon, and Yahoo, and hacked into the systems at Yale and Harvard. In 2001, he pleaded guilty to computer mischief and unauthorized access. He was sentenced to eight months in juvenile detention and probation. Damage to the sites targeted by Mafiaboy was estimated at $7.5 million.

James Ancheta's hacking days ended in 2006. The 20-year-old California computer whiz pleaded guilty to taking control of 400,000 online computers and renting access to them to spammers and fellow hackers. James made more than $100,000 in his scam . . . but also received five years in prison.

In June 2009, Matthew Weigman, a legally blind 19-year-old from Massachusetts, was sentenced to 11 years in prison without parole. Since age 14, Matt hacked into telephone systems to steal credit card information, harass people, cut phone lines, stage a hostage hoax, and fake 911 calls so that SWAT teams would show up at unsuspecting victims' homes (an act known as "swatting"). The FBI had been chasing Matt for years, at times attempting to court him as an informant to help solve other crimes.

> "I TAKE AS A GIVEN THAT YOUNG PEOPLE ARE GOING TO MAKE BAD DECISIONS. NOW IS THE TIME TO CATCH THEM WHEN THE RESULT IS NOT GOING TO BE A FEDERAL INDICTMENT."
> —Principal David Bryan, New Roads School, California

guilty to unauthorized access to a computer security system and the threat charge was dismissed. Cozy was placed on probation in 2008 and ordered to complete 100 community service hours.

United States v. David Kernell (Tennessee, 2008)

In 2008, 20-year-old David C. Kernell was indicted by a federal grand jury in Tennessee for violating the Computer Fraud and Abuse Act. The charges included identification theft, illegal access, and Internet fraud. David, a student at the University of Tennessee, allegedly obtained personal information from the Internet about vice presidential candidate Sarah Palin. He succeeded in changing her password on her Yahoo email account to "popcorn" and read through her messages. He stated that there was "nothing that would derail her campaign as I had hoped." David is facing a maximum of 20 years in prison and a $250,000 fine. His trial is scheduled for April 2010.

> **Not All Hacking Crimes Are Equal**
>
> The penalty for hacking varies from state to state. It depends on a number of factors, including the age of the hacker, the laws that exist in the jurisdiction involved, the amount of damage to the victim, and the hacker's intent and criminal history. A state or federal conviction carries the possibility of restitution, probation, or prison time—even as much as 38 years, as seen in Omar Khan's case (see below).

State v. Omar Khan and Tanvir Singh (California, 2008)

Instead of graduating with his class at Tesoro High School in California in June 2008, 18-year-old Omar Khan sat in jail. Omar and a friend, Tanvir Singh, had broken into the school at night and hacked into the school's computers. They changed test scores from their AP classes and on school records from previous semesters. They also changed the grades of 12 other students and stole tests that they later emailed to others. At one point Omar and Tanvir exchanged text messages about their activities. Omar was in the process of applying to college, and in preparing his transcripts to send out, school administrators noticed all his grades were A's. They became suspicious and started to investigate. The teens were charged with computer fraud, theft, and altering public records.

In September 2008, Tanvir pleaded guilty to illegal computer access and attempting to steal public records. He was placed on three years probation, given 200 community service hours, and ordered to pay restitution to the school. Omar, considered to be the mastermind of the plot, is waiting to go to trial on 69 felony counts—including altering and stealing public records, computer fraud, burglary, identity theft, receiving stolen property, and conspiracy—and faces 38 years in prison.

THINGS TO THINK ABOUT

Why do black hat hackers do what they do? Is it pride or to show off their computer skills? Is it for money or, as you've seen in this chapter, to cheat on tests or change grades? Do you think the hacker considers the long-term effects of being labeled a "hacker" or "cyberbully"? How might this jeopardize future plans for college, military service, or other endeavors? Would you knowingly hire someone who's been in trouble for hacking? Why or why not?

Chapter 15: Further Reading and Resources

Miller, Andrew D. M. "Balancing School Authority and Student Expression." *Baylor Law Review* 54 (Fall 2002): 623.

Pisciotti, Lisa M. "Beyond Sticks and Stones: A First Amendment Framework for Educators Who Seek to Punish Student Threats." *Seton Hall Law Review* 30 (2000): 635.

Ruthven, Fiona. "Is the True Threat the Student or the School Board?" *Iowa Law Review* 88 (April 2003): 931.

CHAPTER 16

When Cyberbullying Turns Deadly

Case: *United States v. Lori Drew* (2008)

Act: creating a fake online profile and using it to harass a neighbor girl who committed suicide as a result

Charge: conspiracy, fraudulent use of the Internet, and providing false information to MySpace

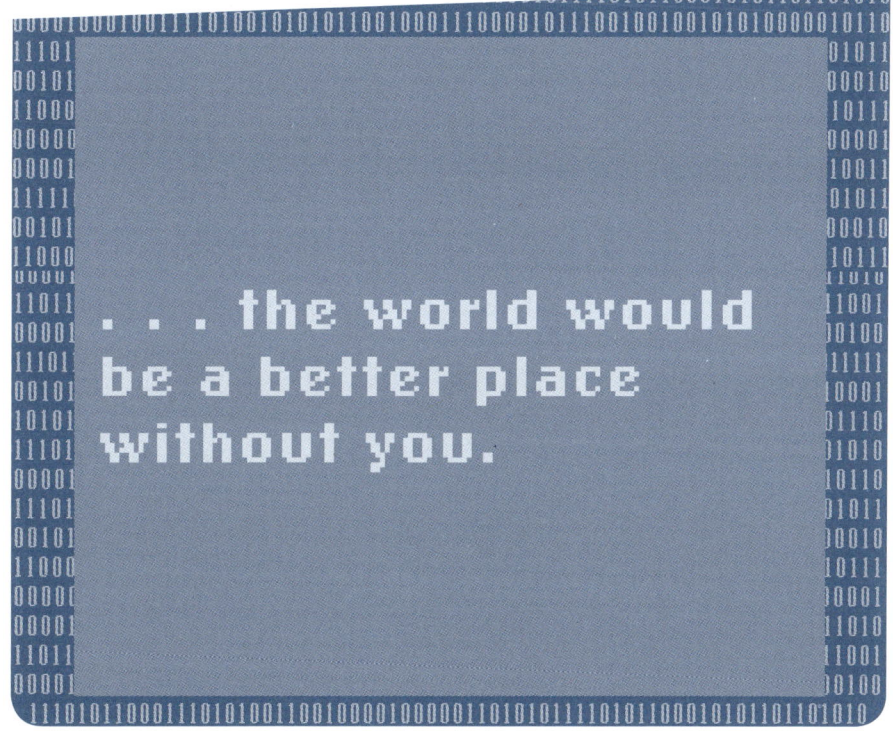

. . . the world would be a better place without you.

Megan Meier was described by her mother as a bubbly and enthusiastic girl who loved hanging out with her dad. She was 13 and in 8th grade at Immaculate Conception School in Missouri. She had struggled with her weight and battled depression. However, she was reportedly upbeat in the fall of 2006.

Megan had recently struck up a relationship with 16-year-old Josh Evans on MySpace. He messaged her and asked to be her friend. Megan agreed and they corresponded for about six weeks. Then Josh turned on Megan, telling her that she was cruel and he didn't want to be her friend anymore. He told her that the world would be a better place without her in it. Other postings found on Josh's site read: "Megan Meier is a slut," and "Megan Meier is fat." Megan's last message to Josh read, "You are the kind of boy a girl would kill herself over." On October 16, 2006, Megan hanged herself with a belt in her bedroom closet and died the next day.

Megan Meier

Megan had been friends with an elementary school classmate who lived down the street. They had been close but grew apart when Megan transferred to a different middle school. The friend's mother, 47-year-old Lori Drew, wanted to know what Megan was saying about her daughter. So Lori and her employee, 18-year-old Ashley Grills, created a fake MySpace profile in order to check up on Megan and gain her trust. In the profile, Lori pretended to be the boy named Josh Evans.

It wasn't until six weeks after Megan's death that the fake profile became known. However, a police investigation did not lead to any charges against Lori Drew, because at the time there were no laws in

Missouri that applied to this situation. Shortly after Megan's suicide, her hometown passed a law that made cyberharassment a crime, but it was not an *ex post facto* law, meaning it did not apply retroactively. Missouri passed a state law in 2008 making cyberbullying a crime, but it also did not apply retroactively.

In May 2008, a federal grand jury in Los Angeles, California, indicted Lori Drew for violating the federal Computer Fraud and Abuse Act. Specifically, she was charged with conspiracy, fraudulent use of the Internet, and providing false information to MySpace when creating Josh's account. When users become MySpace members, they agree to follow specific rules that include not soliciting personal information from anyone under age 18, and not using information gathered from the site to harass, abuse, or harm other people. If Lori were convicted, she could face up to 20 years in prison. Ashley Grills testified against Drew at trial and was granted immunity from prosecution for cooperating with the government.

> An ***ex post facto* law** is one that is retroactive, meaning it applies to something that happened before the law was passed. In Megan's case, cyberbullying became a crime after her death, so any laws against it did not apply to her case.

HOW WOULD YOU DECIDE THIS CASE?

There is no question that Megan's suicide was tragic and may have been avoided. Assuming the final messages from "Josh" drove Megan to end her life, the case raises legal issues regarding free speech and liability for irresponsible Internet writings. Is it wrong or illegal to be cruel? Should you be held accountable for unexpected consequences of your postings, whether in a blog, chat room, or instant message? Where do you draw the line concerning your responsibility to others? What do you think about using someone else's name or creating a fake profile to hide behind?

There are many reasons for remaining anonymous on the Internet. For example, many law enforcement agencies encourage "silent witness" participation in their crime-fighting work. Unless assisting with crime fighting in this way, should you be allowed to remain anonymous while online? The right to speak freely online is important to everyone, including users seeking refuge from abusive spouses, workplace whistleblowers, and government watchdogs.

WHAT THE JURY DECIDED

The charges against Lori Drew were based on the Computer Fraud and Abuse Act, which is a criminal law that carries penalties when violated. It usually applies to Internet hackers who illegally access accounts to get information. This was the first time it had been used to prosecute a person for sending harassing messages and fraudulently attempting to obtain information from a minor.

This was the nation's first criminal cyberbully trial. It was tried before a jury of six men and six women in November 2008. After deliberating for six hours, the jury was hung (meaning no verdict was reached) on the conspiracy charge. Lori Drew was found guilty on the remaining three counts, which were reduced to misdemeanors. This changed a possible 20-year prison sentence to one year in jail and a $100,000 fine on each count. The sentencing court, however, overturned the jury verdicts and acquitted Drew of all charges. The judge said that her actions were not covered by the Computer Fraud law. The government appealed the dismissal of the criminal charges, and in November 2009 withdrew the appeal, ending the case.

> Like Missouri, the majority of U.S. states now have anti-bullying laws. Some have recently added cyberbullying and cyberharassment statutes to their books. See "State, Federal, and European Laws on Cyberbullying" on pages 17–21 for a list of some of those states.

How Does This Case Affect You?

The Internet is a valuable resource and a tremendous social gathering place. Like anything else, however, it can be abused. The suicide of Megan Meier and conviction of Lori Drew (even though it was later overturned) sends a message to all Internet users about lying and bullying and unintended tragic consequences. There is no way to know exactly what another person is thinking or feeling—even your best friend.

The bottom line: Words are powerful. Cruel words may even be fatal. Be mindful of this fact and stop to think before you speak, write, or hit "send."

Megan's mother, Tina Meier, started the Megan Meier Foundation (www.meganmeierfoundation.org) after her daughter's death. Its mission is to promote positive change in response to bullying and cyberbullying. The pledge below was developed in tribute to Megan.

> **The Stop Cyberbullying Pledge***
>
> **By taking this Pledge, I agree to:**
> - Take a stand against cyberbullying, including sharing this pledge with others and asking them to take it too.
> - Not to use technology as a weapon to hurt others.
> - "Think Before I Click."
> - Think about the person on the other side.
> - Support others being cyberbullied and report cyberbullying whenever I find it.
> - Not to join in cyberbullying tactics or be used by cyberbullies to hurt others.
> - "Stop, Block, and Tell" when I am being targeted by a cyberbully and to "Take 5" to help me calm down and walk away from the computer.
> - Be part of the solution, not part of the problem.

* Reprinted with permission from Parry Aftab at Wired Safety Online.

RELATED CASES

State v. Nicole Williams (Missouri, 2008)

In one of the first cases prosecuted under Missouri's 2008 law against cyberbullying, 21-year-old Nicole Williams was charged with harassing a 17-year-old girl. In an argument over a boy, Nicole allegedly left the girl threatening text messages. She referred to the girl as "pork and beans" and threatened her with rape. Nicole pleaded guilty to harassment and was sentenced in 2009 to two years probation and anger management classes.

> "E-THUGS THINK THEY ARE A MILLION TIMES STRONGER BECAUSE THEY CAN HIDE BEHIND THEIR COMPUTER MONITOR."
> —PEW Internet and American Life Project, 2007

In the Matter of Abraham Biggs (Florida, 2008)

Abraham Biggs was a 19-year-old college student with a history of depression. He was on medication and decided to end it all by taking a combination of drugs. Abraham did this in front of a live webcam audience over a 12-hour period in November 2008. Some viewers tried to talk him out of it, while other bloggers encouraged him to continue. Approximately 1,500 viewers watched the streaming video. When the police were finally called and they went to Abraham's apartment, it was too late.

> "[ONLINE COMMUNICATIONS] ARE LIKE THE CROWD OUTSIDE THE BUILDING WITH A GUY ON THE LEDGE. SOMETIMES THERE IS SOMEONE WHO GETS INVOLVED AND TRIES TO TALK HIM DOWN. OFTEN THE CROWD CHANTS, 'JUMP, JUMP.' THEY CAN ENABLE SUICIDE OR HELP PREVENT IT."
> —Professor Jeffrey Cole, University of Southern California, 2008

In the Matter of Rachael Neblett (Kentucky, 2006)

Rachael was a friendly 17-year-old student at Bullitt High School in Kentucky. She was a cheerleader and excelled in gymnastics. She had a passion for lipgloss and sunglasses.

Rachael Neblett

In the summer of 2006, she started receiving threatening emails at home. Rachael believed the sender to be another student because she knew where Rachael was during the day at school. Rachael didn't tell her parents right away, but she did share the emails with her sisters and friends. The principal was notified and he and Rachael's teachers kept an eye on Rachael. In September 2006, she received the following message:

"Meet me out front of school . . . and we'll settle it there and honey you are not going to the hospital. I'm going to put you in the morgue."

According to her father, Rachael was petrified. She stopped her daily activities out of fear and stayed home when not in class. Three weeks later she shot herself in the chest in her parents' bedroom and died. The police investigation to identify Rachael's cyberstalker continues. It is believed that someone was threatening Rachael through a fake MySpace account.

In an unexpected turn of events, six months after Rachael's death, her close friend committed suicide. In April 2007, 16-year-old Kristin Settles, who was devastated by Rachael's passing, hanged herself. She left a note asking that she be buried next to Rachael. Kristin's story may be read on the Make a Difference for Kids Web site listed above.

> **Make a Difference for Kids**
> Rachael Neblett's father started a nonprofit group dedicated to spreading an anti-bullying, anti-suicide message. Visit www.makeadifferenceforkids.org.

In the Matter of Jeffrey Johnston (Florida, 2005)

Jeff Johnston stood out not only because he was almost six feet tall, but because of his shoulder-length hair. He was growing it out to donate to Locks of Love, a charity for cancer patients. After breaking up with a girl when he was in 7th grade, he was called a stalker and was bullied online for the next three years. When he was in 8th grade, someone hacked into his online video game and filled it with nasty comments.

Jeffrey Johnston

Cyber-Bullycide Across the Globe

South Korea
Nearly 200,000 cases of cyberviolence were reported in 2007 in South Korea. "Our Internet culture is more violent and vicious than most other countries. People don't respect each other in cyberspace," says communications professor Youngchul Yoon of Seoul's Yonsei University. In October 2008, 39-year-old Choi Jin-sil, one of South Korea's most popular movie stars, hanged herself in her shower at home. She was nicknamed "The Nation's Actress" but was hounded by thousands of chat-room users attacking her morals and character. In response, the South Korean police cracked down on abusive Internet use. Several thousand people were arrested for spreading malicious rumors online, libel, and cyberstalking. Then South Korea passed a law that requires Web users to reveal their real names and government issued ID number when posting to sites such as Google and YouTube.

> South Korea now has a law that requires Web users to reveal their real names and government issued ID number when posting to social networking sites.

England
Sam Leeson was bullied online for his interest in the emo subculture. (Emos often wear long bangs, skinny pants, and listen to angst-ridden music.)

At age 15, Jeff wrote, "the world would never change" and "I'll never get over 8th grade." Not long after leaving these notes in his bedroom, Jeff hanged himself in his closet. Jeff's death brought about Florida's "Jeffrey Johnston Stand Up for Students Act," which requires public schools to implement anti-bullying policies. Visit www.jeffreyjohnston.org for more information.

> "A BULLY DOESN'T HAVE TO BE EYE TO EYE TO BULLY SOMEONE. SOMETIMES HE OR SHE GETS INTO CYBERSPACE AND THEN THERE'S NO PLACE TO HIDE FROM THEIR TORMENT."
> — Debbie Johnston, Jeff's mother

In June 2008, the 13-year-old ended his life by hanging himself at home in England.

In 2009, 15-year-old Megan Gillan of Macclesfield High School in England was tormented on her Bebo Web page by classmates about her appearance and "scabby" clothes. The school and her parents tried to protect her from the bullies but were unsuccessful. She took a fatal dose of painkillers after texting a friend, "I love you, never forget that." Megan's friends made a video tribute to her, which can be found here: www.youtube.com/watch?v=wwhYhqgE0es.

When the bullying became unbearable, 15-year-old Holly Grogan of Gloucester, England, switched to a private school. But the bullies followed her. She endured a torrent of abusive comments on her Facebook wall. Holly's close friend, Chloe, said that girls would gang up on her and call her names. Holly "didn't have anything to say back—she just froze up." In September 2009, Holly jumped 30 feet to her death from a bridge into traffic.

Japan

In July 2007, an 18-year-old boy jumped to his death at his high school in Japan. Classmates had posted a nude photo of him on a Web site and repeatedly sent him emails demanding money. Several classmates were arrested.

In the Matter of Ryan Patrick Halligan (Vermont, 2003)

Ryan was in middle school in Vermont. He loved acting and comedy. He was not athletic and struggled with his grades. When Ryan was 11, kids started picking on him at school. His parents let him take kickboxing lessons to build his confidence. While in 7th grade, Ryan confronted one bully and got in a few swings before the vice principal broke up the fight. Then he and the bully became friends for a short time until the bully turned on him by spreading online rumors that Ryan was gay.

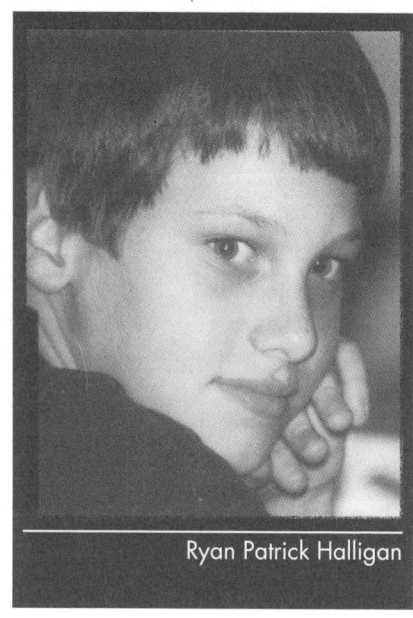

Ryan Patrick Halligan

During the following summer, Ryan instant messaged a girl he had a crush on. Later at school she told him she was just pretending to like him and that he was a loser. Not long after, Ryan waited for his family to go to sleep before he went into the bathroom and hanged himself. He was 13 years old.

Since Ryan's death, his father, John Halligan, has become an advocate and educator regarding cyberbullying laws. At a conference on cyberbullying in November 2008, Mr. Halligan spoke to 300 middle and high school students. Jed, age 13, commented that, "After hearing Ryan's story, it just goes to show how much one thing, one sentence, can do to hurt a family. Just like that."

Important! If you or someone you know is being harassed online, experiencing depression, or having suicidal thoughts, talk to a parent, counselor, teacher, or other trusted adult as soon as possible. Or contact one of the organizations listed in the front of this book.

In the Matter of Ricky Alatorre (Indiana, 2008)

Ricky Alatorre was a heavyset 16-year-old who lived on his family's farm in Indiana and did well in school. While Ricky was in English class in 2008, a classmate secretly took his picture. Soon a fake profile titled "The Rictionary" showed up on MySpace that claimed that Ricky was gay and loved dictionaries, and poked fun at his high grades at school.

"I was completely devastated," Ricky said. "It's one thing if it's in my school paper because that's contained within a small area. But when you put it on the Internet, you are opening up to everyone in the world." Upon request, MySpace removed the profile from the Web.

"I had thought about suicide," Ricky said. "It looked very welcoming at certain times." With the help of his family and the school, Ricky is coping with more than the usual growing pains.

Billy Wolfe v. John Doe (Arkansas, 2008)

Billy Wolfe attended Fayetteville High School in Arkansas. As a 15-year-old sophomore, he put up with school bullies since he was 12. That's when he received a call at home asking if he was interested in buying a sex toy. He told his mother, who reported it to the other kids' parents. The next day Billy saw a list of 20 kids who wanted to beat him up.

Billy is tall and thin and has a learning disability. He likes the outdoors, racquetball, and girls. Over a three-year period he endured assaults at school, on the school bus, and in class. One attack was recorded on a cell phone camera and posted on the Internet. A Facebook page called "Everyone That Hates Billy Wolfe" invited others to beat up Billy. In response to this site, others were created like "Not Everyone Hates Billy Wolfe," and "Not Cool, Billy Wolfe Haters." Each of these sites drew hundreds of supporters.

In September 2008, Billy sued the school and assistant principal for failing to protect him from physical and online harassment. He alleged that the school did not discipline the students who bullied him. He was quoted saying he just wants "to get kids to leave me alone and stop bullying me." Billy graduated in 2009. His lawsuit remains pending at the time of this book's publication.

Hailee Wiggins-Ketchum v. Corona del Mar High School (2009)

Hailee was a 17-year-old senior at Corona del Mar High in California. In January 2009, she became the online victim of four varsity athletes at school. They posted a video on Facebook in which they threatened to rape Hailee in the back of a pickup truck, and then acted out how they would shoot her to death.

Hailee's parents reported the threats to the school and the police. Little was done. The boys were suspended for a few days, and a few months later the school honored them for their athletic prowess. No criminal charges were filed. In the meantime, Hailee was forced to change her personal and school schedule to avoid contact with the boys.

Hailee and her parents sued the school district for allowing a sexist, homophobic, and intolerant atmosphere to flourish at the school. In September 2009, a settlement was reached. The school district agreed to write a letter of apology to Hailee. They further agreed to implement a training program for all school administrators, teachers, and students that focuses on the harmful impact of sexual discrimination and harassment.

Upon reaching the agreement, Hailee commented that, "I hope other students will learn from my experiences that it is possible to stand up for what is right and to prevail."

THINGS TO THINK ABOUT

Do you think people are so desensitized by violent videos, computer games, television, and movies that watching a teenager slowly kill himself causes few to react? Is using a fake profile to harass or bully someone acceptable behavior? Do you have a friend who is being bullied, online or off? Do you feel any responsibility to get involved, or is it easier to pretend it's nothing and everything will be okay? Do you realize that you can't hide behind your computer screen—that a social networking site may either agree to or be court-ordered to disclose your real name? Think about these points and discuss them with friends and family.

Chapter 16: Further Reading and Resources

Bullying, No Way • www.bullyingnoway.com.au
Australia's educational communities reach out to students with "talk out" opportunities, "chill out space," and more.

Childnet International • www.childnet.com
This nonprofit organization publishes powerful DVDs, posters, and other materials to reach out to bullied teens.

Ryan's Story • www.ryanpatrickhalligan.org
Ryan Halligan was in 8th grade when online bullying lead to his suicide. Visit this memorial Web site for information and resources regarding bullying and suicide prevention.

SafeKids.com • www.safekids.com/family-contract-for-online-safety
Help establish Internet rules you and your parents can both agree on. Visit this Web site for example contracts.

Suicide.org • www.suicide.org
Resources, forums, and hotlines for suicide prevention, awareness, and support. For state, national, and international hotlines, click on "Suicide Prevention Hotlines."

Closing Statement

You have finished reading a variety of cases involving different aspects of communication. The Internet, cell phones, and all methods of electronic contact were never intended to be used as weapons. However, as you have seen, there are consequences—sometimes severe ones—for those who carelessly use or abuse modern technology.

- What, if anything, have you learned from these stories?
- Are you surprised by the outcomes of some of the cases? Which ones, and why?
- Were you aware that a simple online post or text message could have such far-reaching effects?
- Do you feel that the courts fairly balanced the issues in each case? If not, which cases do you feel were handled unfairly and why?
- Should courts become more involved with the daily activities at school? Why or why not?
- Are you surprised by the number of decisions in favor of the student—even when a student's speech was offensive or inappropriate? If so, which decisions surprised you and why?
- Do you think courts do all they can to protect students' individual rights? Why or why not?
- Were you surprised to learn that teachers have rights, too, and can sue a student for injuries and loss?

The responsibility of the judicial system is to strengthen the First Amendment and avoid disturbing the exercise of speaking freely. Protecting this freedom for young people in the digital age requires a delicate balance between student speech and the rights of others. As you now know from these cases, courts disagree and decisions can go one way or another. As one federal judge wrote in 2009, "when it comes to student cyberspeech, the lower courts are in complete disarray." It won't be long before the U.S. Supreme Court steps in and provides direction in this new era.

Until then, keep these cases in mind and, in the words of The Stop Cyberbullying Pledge, remember to always **think before you click**.

How to Do Legal Research

Can you envision adding to your term paper one of the easy-to-find resources listed in this book? By following the simple instructions offered here, you can find the actual court opinions in these cases, law review articles, and other cited publications. Public libraries, law libraries, and the Internet can assist in your research. If you get stuck, ask a reference librarian who will be happy to help you.

COURT OPINIONS

The published opinions of all of the country's appellate courts are found in a series of books called reporters. The series is divided into regions—for example, California decisions are found in the *Pacific Reporter,* and Maine decisions are located in the *Atlantic Reporter.* Each state also maintains its own set of reporters. This means that each decision may be found in both a regional and a state reporter. The decisions of the United States Supreme Court can be found in several federal reporters. All of the Supreme Court cases cited in this book are located in either the *U.S. Supreme Court Reports* or the *Supreme Court Reporter.*

Regional and Federal Reporters, with Abbreviations

<u>Regional Reporters</u>
Atlantic Reporter (A.)
Northwest Reporter (N.W.)
Northeast Reporter (N.E.)
Southern Reporter (So.)
Southwest Reporter (S.W.)
Southeast Reporter (S.E.)
Pacific Reporter (P.)

<u>Federal Reporters</u>
Federal Reporter (F.)
Federal Supplement (F.Supp.)
U.S. Supreme Court Reports (U.S.)
Supreme Court Reporter (S.Ct.)

Note: A "2d" or "3d" following any of these abbreviations means second or third series, which is printed on the side of the volume.

Each published opinion is assigned a citation number. For example, if you want to read the full opinion of the U.S. Supreme Court in *Tinker v. Des Moines Independent Community School District* (1969), start with the case citation, which is 393 U.S. 503 (1969). This means you can find the opinion in volume 393 of the *U.S. Supreme Court Reports* on page 503; 1969 refers to the year of the decision.

Regarding state court opinions, consider the case of *J.S. v. Bethlehem School District* (2002). Its citation number is 807 A.2d 847 (2002). Its published opinion may be found in volume 807 of the *Atlantic Reporter* (abbreviated "A.") second series ("2d"), on page 847. This was a Pennsylvania case and is also reported in that state's reporter series in 569 Pa. 638 (volume 569 of the *Pennsylvania Reports*, page 638).

You can find information on some cases—particularly Supreme Court cases—on the Internet. Go to Justia News at www.justia.com, FindLaw at www.findlaw.com, or Citizen Media Law Project at www.citmedialaw.org. The information is public, which means you don't have to be a judge, lawyer, or law student to obtain the material.

LEGAL ARTICLES

The legal articles cited in this book usually list the name of the journal publishing the article, the author, a volume number followed by the page number, and the year the article was written. Locate the article in a law library or online. If you visit the publication's Web site, you should be able to locate the article by searching for the volume and page number. You might also find the article by doing a Google search of the title or author's name.

Many law libraries are located on college campuses. If there isn't a law library in your area, you can write or call the nearest one, whether in your state or a neighboring state. Provide the name and citation of the case or article you'd like, so a librarian can assist you. You may have to pay a small fee for photocopies.

Glossary of Terms

Acceptable Use Policy (AUP). A written statement by a school declaring its policy of acceptable uses of the school's computers and penalties for violations. The policy is usually found in a school's student handbook.

Actual Damages. Money awarded to compensate a person for real, proven injuries he or she suffered.

Appeal. The right to ask a higher court, called an appellate court, to review a decision made by a lower court. This is done by reading a transcript of what took place in the lower court, and listening to the oral arguments of the attorneys involved. The attorneys may also file written arguments about their case called *briefs*.

Bash Board. An online bulletin board where individuals can post anything they want. The term "bash" is used because oftentimes the messages directed at another person are hateful and malicious.

Blocking. When you are denied access to part of the Internet. Usually a message will appear notifying you of such.

Blog. An interactive online journal or diary, viewable by designated friends or everyone. The blogger adds content to his or her Web log by blogging.

Botnet. A collection of infected computers used to steal a person's identity and personal information.

Buddy List. A collection of names of your friends or "buddies" within an instant message or chat program. You can see when they are online and available to talk, and they can see when you are online.

Bullycide. Suicide stemming directly or indirectly from being bullied or cyberbullied—usually an act of depression, desperation, and loneliness.

Bullying. Harmful behavior against another person usually of a repetitive nature—it may include physical or psychological acts of aggression.

Censorship. The act of limiting access to material found objectionable; for example, books, movies, and music with explicit sexual content, violence, or profanity.

Chat. An online conversation in a "chat room" where you can read others' messages and they can read your replies. Some chat rooms have hundreds of participants online at once, having real-time conversations.

Cyberbullying. The use of electronic devices such as computers and cell phones to convey intimidating or harassing messages (i.e., text or IM messages, graphic harassment, and email).

Cyberdating. Following up an online relationship with an off-line real date.

Cyberthreats. Electronic messages that indicate an intention to do harm to yourself or another.

Damages. A remedy in the form of money to the injured person—also see *actual*, *nominal*, and *punitive* damages.

Defamation. A false statement of fact, written or oral, that is communicated to a third party and injures one's reputation.

Delinquent. When a minor is found guilty of a crime, he or she is called a *delinquent* child, not a criminal. If found guilty of truancy, running away, or disobedience, the minor is referred to as an *incorrigible* child.

Digital Footprint. Anything that can be traced to your use of the Internet, including a deleted or trashed email, blog, or chat entry.

Due Process. Your constitutional right under the Fourteenth Amendment to be notified of any charge filed against you and be given a chance to respond to the charge.

Email. Stands for "electronic mail"; allows you to receive and send messages to other Internet users.

Email Bomb. A form of Internet abuse where someone sends huge volumes of email to an address in an attempt to fill their mailbox or overload a server.

Emoticon. From "emotion" and "icon"; a way for Internet users to express an emotion behind a word or sentence. A common emoticon is a smiley face ☺.

Ex Post Facto Law. A law that applies to a person or event before the law was passed, in other words, a law that applies retroactively.

Expunge. To have your juvenile record erased, as if it never existed. This allows you to begin your adult life (age 18) with a clean record.

Facebook. A popular social networking Web site where users create personal profiles of themselves, listing interests, communicating with others, and posting photos.

Felony. A crime that carries the strictest penalty, usually a minimum of one year in jail. A felony is more serious than a *misdemeanor* or a *petty offense*.

Flaming. The practice of sending rude, angry, or obscene messages to someone.

Friending. Adding another user to your list of friends on a social networking site such as Facebook or MySpace.

Grand Jury. A group of citizens who decide whether enough evidence is available to charge someone with a crime. They listen to the government's evidence presented by a prosecutor behind closed doors. Unlike a criminal trial that is open to the public, grand jury proceedings are closed hearings. They usually deal with felonies, not misdemeanors or lesser crimes. If the grand jury finds sufficient evidence against the person, they issue a formal charge called an *indictment*.

Hacking. Breaking into a computer or computer system without permission.

Happy Slapping. An extreme form of bullying where physical assaults are recorded on cell phones or other devices and posted on the Internet.

Harassment. When a person is the victim of unsolicited words or actions intended to alarm, abuse, or annoy them.

Hate Speech. Speech intended to degrade or disparage someone or a group based on race, gender, religion, sexual orientation, ethnicity, or other improper classification.

Hung Jury. A jury that cannot agree on a decision in the case. This usually happens after hours or even days of considering the evidence, and it means that the case may be retried.

Incorrigible. An incorrigible act is one that cannot be committed by an adult, such as running away, truancy, and disobedience. If the court finds you incorrigible, you could be placed on probation.

Indictment. A formal charge against a person for committing a crime, brought against him or her by a grand jury.

Instant Messaging (IM). An act of instant communication between two or more people over the Internet. Programs such as AOL Instant Messenger or Google Talk allow this to occur.

Internet. A massive worldwide network of computers communicating with each other by use of phone lines, satellite links, wireless networks, and cable systems. The Internet isn't owned by anyone and does not have a specific location. A large portion of the Internet is called the World Wide Web.

Libel. The publication, in words, photos, pictures, or symbols, of false statements of fact that harm another's reputation (i.e., in a Web page or blog post). The absolute defense to a charge of libel is the truth.

Minor. Someone who is not yet legally an adult—in most situations, someone 17 or younger.

Misdemeanor. A criminal offense that is less serious than a felony, and results in a fine, probation, or a jail sentence of one year or less.

MySpace. A social networking Web site that allows the user to create a personal online profile. It may include biographical information, interests, likes and dislikes, pictures, video, and audio. A user interacts with others through blogging, messaging, or posting comments.

Negligence. Occurs when a person fails to exercise the care that a reasonable person would exercise under the same circumstances.

Nominal Damages. A small amount of money ($1.00 or $10.00, for example) awarded by a court recognizing a successful claim in a lawsuit but with little monetary merit.

Petty Offense. A criminal offense that usually carries no jail time and a low fine.

Phishing. Illegally attempting to acquire sensitive information such as usernames, passwords, and credit card details by masquerading as a trustworthy entity in an electronic communication.

Probable Cause. Exists when the facts and circumstances within an officer's knowledge are sufficient in themselves to cause a person of reasonable caution to believe that an offense has been or is being committed.

Probation. A program in which you're supervised by the court or probation department for a period of time. Special terms of probation may include time in detention, community service hours, counseling, a fine, or restitution to the victim.

Profile. A user created Web page where you add content including your background, interests, and friends. You can also add music, video, and digital pictures.

Punitive Damages. Money awarded to an injured plaintiff in a lawsuit that is considered punishment for willful behavior, in order to set an example for others.

Reasonable Doubt. In a criminal trial the court or jury must find that the case has been proven "beyond a reasonable doubt." This means that there may still be a doubt, as long as it doesn't affect a reasonable person's belief that the person on trial is guilty. It is the highest level of persuasion that must be met in a criminal case.

Restitution. The act of restoring a victim to the position he or she was in before suffering property damage, loss, or personal injury. A minor placed on probation may be required to pay back the victim for any loss the minor caused. Payments may be spread out over the length of the probation period.

Right to Privacy. Control over your personal information and the ability to grant or deny access to others. It is your right to decide how much you will share with others about your thoughts, feelings, and the facts of your life.

Sexting. Sending graphic images or sexually explicit photos or videos by way of text messages to friends.

Slander. A defamatory statement made against another person.

Social Networking Web Site. An interactive online environment where users share their profiles, blogs, photos, and messages. Some popular sites include MySpace, Facebook, Bebo, LiveJournal, Xanga, PhotoBucket, and Flickr.

Spam. The same as "junk mail" from the post office; unsolicited email from someone you don't know.

Statute of Limitations. A law that states the maximum period of time after a certain event that you can file a lawsuit (e.g., one, two, or three years).

Swatting. Telephone hacking often used to make false 911 calls to get SWAT teams to respond to an unsuspecting person's home, while the "swatter" observes nearby. This is a form of harassment.

Teacher Baiting. The act of intentionally upsetting a teacher so that he or she says or does something that a student catches on video in order to post online.

Texting. Sending a written message to someone over your cell phone.

Trolling. When someone sends out an anonymous message in an attempt to get you to respond; often done to upset or provoke the receiver.

True Threat. A statement communicated as a serious expression of an intention to inflict bodily harm upon or take the life of another person. True threats are not protected by the U.S. Constitution and may be criminal.

Twitter. A social networking service used as a way to stay connected with your friends online with quick answers, called *tweets*, to the question "What are you doing?" Described as bite-size updates or micro-blogging and limited to 140 characters.

Wikipedia. A free online encyclopedia with entries called *wikis*, created and edited by users.

YouTube. A video-sharing Web site where users can upload, view, and share clips of themselves or others.

Additional Web Resources

The following Web sites were used in the research for this book. Each provides current information about cases involving student free expression online and offline. Most sites offer an opportunity to sign up for email alerts or news feeds.

www.aclu.org • The mission of the American Civil Liberties Union is to protect individuals' First Amendment rights, their right to equal protection under the law, their right to due process of law, and their right to privacy. The ACLU represented some of the persons in this book in their pursuit of justice. Search on student issues for youth news and opportunities to participate.

www.askthejudge.info • Ask the Judge is an interactive Web site about the legal rights of children and teens. It features current events, blogs, and over 100 questions and answers about young people and the law.

www.athinline.org • MTV's A Thin Line campaign was developed to empower kids and teens to identify, respond to, and stop the spread of digital abuse in their lives. Take the quiz, get the facts, take control, and share your story.

www.cjcj.org • The Center on Juvenile and Criminal Justice offers public education and research in fields of juvenile and criminal justice.

www.cyberbullying.us • The Cyberbullying Research Center is an information clearinghouse for identifying the causes and consequences of online harassment.

www.edweek.org • Education Week provides the latest important K–12 news from across the nation.

www.eschoolnews.com • eSchool News offers a daily recap of education news regarding technology and Internet issues involving students and teachers.

www.firstamendmentcenter.org • The First Amendment Center provides comprehensive coverage of First Amendment issues including coverage of U.S. Supreme Court cases and analysis.

www.justia.com • Justia Company provides case law and legal articles about current court challenges and the outcome of each.

www.govtrack.us • GovTrack helps you follow bills in the U.S. Congress. Sign up to track pending legislation of interest to you.

www.oyez.org • Oyez (meaning "to hear") is a multimedia Web site where you can listen to the oral arguments of the U.S. Supreme Court, take a virtual tour of the Court building, and learn about current justices.

www.splc.org • The Student Press Law Center is an advocate for student free-press rights and provides information, advice, and legal assistance to students and the educators who work with them.

www.supremecourtus.gov • The United States Supreme Court Web site includes the Court's history, biographies of current justices, recent cases, opinions, and oral argument schedules and transcripts.

www.upfrontmagazine.com • Published by *The New York Times* and Scholastic, *Upfront* is a news magazine for teens highlighting current events, including those involving law and the Internet.

Sources

Introduction

Internet use facts on page 1 are from: Nielsen Online, July 2009; Center for the Digital Future, University of Southern California report, November 2008; PEW Internet and American Life Project, 2007–2008; and *South Coast Today*, June 1, 2009.

Cyberbullying facts on page 3 are from: The Cyber Safety and Ethics Initiative/Rochester Institute of Technology Report, November 2008; www.wiredsafety.org; and www.pewinternet.org.

Quote from Professor Juvonen on page 3 is from: Juvonen, Jaana, and Elisheva Gross. "Extending the School Grounds? Bullying Experiences in Cyberspace." *Journal of School Health* 78 (September 2008): 496.

Part I: Cyberbullying and the Law

Quote from the Supreme Court of Wisconsin on page 10 is from: *State ex rel. Dresser v. District Board of School District No. 1*, 135 Wis. 619, 116 NW 232 (1908). The suspension would end when the girls apologized and each paid the school a 40-cent fine.

Quote from the U.S. Supreme Court on page 11 is from: *West Virginia Board of Education v. Barnette*, 319 U.S. 624 (1943).

The following court cases are referenced on pages 11–15:
In re Gault, 387 U.S. 1 (1967); *Tinker v. Des Moines Independent Community School District*, 393 U.S. 503 (1969); *Wood v. Strickland*, 420 U.S. 308 (1975); *Bethel School District No. 403 v. Fraser*, 478 U.S. 675 (1986); *Hazelwood School District v. Kuhlmeier*, 484 U.S. 260 (1988); *Morse v. Frederick*, 127 S.Ct. 2618 (2007).

Quote from U.S. Supreme Court on page 15 is from: *Reno v. ACLU*, 521 U.S. 844 (1997).

The Interstate Communications Law is from: 18 United States Code 875(c) (1948).

The Protecting Children in the 21st Century Act is from: 47 United States Code 157, Section 101; Public Law 110-385.

The California 2008 law regarding foster children is from: California Health and Safety Code Sec. 1529.2 and Welfare and Institutions Code Sec. 16003.

Chapter 1
Featured case: *Justin Swidler v. Bethlehem Area School District*, 807 A.2d 847 (Pennsylvania, 2002).

Fighting words case on page 31: *Chaplinsky v. State of New Hampshire*, 315 U.S. 568 (1942).

Chapter 2
Featured case: *Zachariah Paul v. Franklin Regional School District*, 136 F.Supp.2d 446 (Pennsylvania, 2001).

Email fact on page 38 and safety tips on page 39 are from: PEW Internet and American Life Project, 2009.

Chapter 3
Featured case: *Justin Layshock v. Hermitage School District*, 2007 West Law 2022096 (Pennsylvania, 2007).

Social networking stats on pages 50–51 are from: Minnesota College of Education and Human Development, 2008; and PEW Internet and American Life Project, October 24, 2007.

Chapter 4
Featured case: *A.B. v. State of Indiana*, 885 N.E.2d 1223 (Indiana Supreme Court, 2008).

MySpace study details on page 57 are from: Moreno, Megan A., and others. "Reducing At-Risk Adolescents' Display of Risk Behavior on a Social Networking Web Site." *Archives of Pediatrics and Adolescent Medicine* 163:1 (January 2009).

Social networking safety tips on page 59 are from: Kaplan Education, 2008.

Chapter 5
Featured case: *Avery Doninger v. Lewis Mills High School*, 527 F.3d 41 (2nd Circuit Court of Appeals, Connecticut, 2008).

The Family Educational Rights and Privacy Act information is from: 20 U.S. Code Sec. 1232g.

Fact about blogging on page 66 is from: PEW Internet and American Life Project, 2009.

Facts about the benefits of blogging on pages 66–67 are from: *Miami Herald*, November 9, 2008; PEW Internet and American Life Project, April 24, 2008; and Professor Nenagh Kemp, University of Tasmania, Australia, 2008.

Quote from Justin Reich on page 68 is from: Reich, Justin. "Turn Teen Texting Toward Better Writing." *Christian Science Monitor* (May 13, 2008).

Chapter 6
Featured case: *Ian Michael Lake v. State of Utah*, 61 P.3d 1038 (Utah Supreme Court, 2002).

Facts in "Have You Googled Yourself Lately?" on page 77 are from: Epstein, Dina. "Have I Been Googled? Character and Fitness in the Age of Google, Facebook and YouTube." *21 Georgetown Journal of Legal Ethics* 715 (Summer, 2008).

Chapter 7
Featured case: *Gregory Requa v. Kent School District*, 92 F.Supp.2d 1272 (Washington, 2007).

Fact about New York cell phone ban on page 85 is from: *Price v. New York City Board of Education*, 16 Misc.3d 543 (2008).

Sexting facts on page 88 are from: Teenage Research Unlimited survey, October 2008; The National Center for Missing and Exploited Children report, December 2008.

Reminders to avoid sexting on page 91 are adapted in part from: CosmoGirl.com, October 2008.

Chapter 8
Featured case: *Jon Coy v. Canton City Schools*, 205 F.Supp.2d 791 (Ohio, 2002).

Facts in "Cyberbullying Is on the Rise" on page 98 are from: University of New Hampshire's Crimes Against Children Research Center (2008); Public Health Agency of Canada, 2009; Microsoft Canada and Youthography Internet Safety Survey, February 2009; and University of Queensland, 2008.

Chapter 9
Featured case: *Joshua Mahaffey v. Waterford School District*, 236 F.Supp.2d 779 (Michigan, 2002).

Chapter 10
Featured case: *Nick Emmett v. Kent School District*, 92 F.Supp.2d 1088 (Eastern District, Washington, 2000).

Chapter 11
Featured case: *Aaron Wisniewski v. Weedsport Central School District*, 494 F.3d 34 (2nd Circuit Court of Appeals, New York, 2007). Appeal to the U.S. Supreme Court was denied on March 31, 2008: 128 S.Ct. 1741.

IM and texting facts on page 118 are from: PEW Internet and American Life Project, 2009; *Upfront Magazine*, October 20, 2008; and the U.S. Justice Department, February 2009.

Chapter 12
Featured case: *State v. Joshua Mortimer*, 542 S.E.2d 330 (North Carolina, 2001).

Chapter 13
Featured case: *Jack Flaherty Jr. v. Keystone Oaks School District*, 47 F.Supp.2d 698 (W.D. Pa., 2003).

Quote from Thierry Guedj on page 135 is from: Brown, Edward. "Cyberbullying on the Rise, on Campus," *BU Today* Web exclusive: www.bu.edu/bostonia/web/cyberbullying (accessed April 11, 2014).

Chapter 14
Featured case: *Ryan Dwyer v. Oceanport School District*, unpublished opinion, U.S. Dist. Ct. New Jersey, March 31, 2005.

Chapter 15
Featured case: *Justin Boucher v. School District of Greenfield*, 134 F.3d 821 (1998).

Fact about cybercheating on page 152 is from: The Josephson Institute of Ethics in California.

Information about government white hat hackers on page 152 is from: *e-School News*, May 2, 2009.

Chapter 16
Featured case: *United States v. Lori Drew*, Case No. CR-08-582-GW, U.S. District Court (California, 2008).

Closing Statement
Quote on page 171 is from: *Avery Doninger v. Niehoff*, 2009 West Law 1364890, U.S. District Court (Connecticut, May 2009).

Index

A

Aaron Wisniewski v. Weedsport Central School District (New York, 2007), 115–117
A.B. v. State of Indiana (2008), 53–56
Acceptable Use Policy (AUP), 94–96, 136, 149
Actual damages, defined, 174
Addiction to Internet, 104–105
Alatorre, Ricky, 167
Alpert, Phillip, 87
Ancheta, James, 153
Antony Latour v. Riverside Beaver School District (Pennsylvania, 2005), 112
Appeal, defined, 174
Appellate courts, 9
Avery Doninger v. Lewis Mills High School (Connecticut, 2008), 61–65, 67

B

Bayer, Peter, 76
Beidler, Karl, 32–33
Bemis, Pat, 132
Beussink, Brandon, 41
Biggs, Abraham, 162
Billy Wolfe v. John Doe (Arkansas, 2008), 167
Black hat hackers, 151
Blogs, 61–67, 143, 162
Boucher, Justin, 147–151
Bowler, Christopher, 97
Bozzuto, Robert, 36, 37
Brandon Beussink v. Woodland School District (Missouri, 1998), 41
Broadband Data Improvement Act (2008), 18

C

Canada, 119
Cell phones, 68, 85, 98
  See also Text messages; Video clips
Censorship, defined, 175
Child pornography, 86–89
Children. *See* Young people
China, 104
Choi Jin-sil, 164
Christopher Bowler v. Hudson High School (Massachusetts, 2004), 97
Civil libel, 72
Civil liberties, protecting (Web site), 69
Codes of conduct
  AUPs, 94–96, 136, 149
  location of incident and, 126–127
  vagueness of, 132–134

Colleges and Internet, 59, 67
Columbine High School, 8, 124
Communications Decency Act (1996), 18, 75, 141
Computer Fraud and Abuse Act, 154, 159, 160
Conradt, Brian, 106–107
Court system. *See* Judicial system
Coy, Jon, 93–97
Creative expression
  with disclaimers, 109–111
  graphic arts, 112, 113, 115–118, 119–120
  music, 112–113, 118–119
Criminal libel, 71–74
Curzon-Brown, Daniel, 144
Curzon-Brown v. Lathouwer (California, 2000), 143–144
Cyberbullies, characteristics of, 2
Cyberbullying
  blocking content, 120
  examples of, 2–3
  increase in, 98
  pledge to stop, 161
  tips for dealing with, 43, 98, 100
  Web sites about, 100, 169
  young people victimized statistics, xi, 3
Cyber-cheating, 152–153
Cyber security, 136, 152
Cyprus, 85
Czech Republic, 1, 85

D

Dan Sullivan v. Houston Independent School District (Texas, 1973), 58
Defamation, 175
  See also Libel
Denise E. Finkel v. Facebook & Others (New York, 2009), 75
Doninger, Avery, 15, 61–65, 67
Doninger v. Niehoff (Connecticut, 2009), 15
Dougherty, Andy, 86–87
Draker, Anna, 49–50
Draker v. Schreiber (Texas, 2008), 49–50
Dresser, Hazel and Mabel, case of (Wisconsin, 1908), 10
Drew, Lori, 157–160
Due process rights, 37, 78, 176
Duffin, Cyd, 49–50
Dustin Mitchell v. Rolla Public Schools (Missouri, 1999), 126–127
Dwyer, Ryan, 139–143

E

Eckhardt, 11–12
Elder people and blogging, 66
Electronic message board postings, 131–135
Ellison, Reid, 152

Email
  benefits of, 66–67, 104
  hacking into accounts, 154
  privacy of, 35–39
  teen usage statistics, 38
  threats, 31, 163
  tips for using safely, 39
Emmett, Nick, 109–111
England, 77, 164–165
Ethics, 16–17, 42
Evans, Katherine, 76
Ex post facto laws, 159, 176

F

Facebook, 51
  See also Social networking sites
Faculty. *See* School personnel
Fake profiles, cases with
  Draker, 49–50
  in foreign countries, 2
  Jill Snyder, 77
  John Doe, 76
  Justin Layshock, 45–48
  In the Matter of Ricky Alatorre, 167
  United States v. Lori Drew, 157–160
Family Educational Rights and Privacy
  Act (1974), 64
Federal government
  court system, 9
  cyber security, 152
  laws, 18, 64
  Supreme Court, 121, 172–173
Felony, defined, 176
Finkel, Denise E., 75
Finland, 1, 86–87
First Amendment
  false statements and, 73
  judicial system responsibility to, 171
  limits on free speech rights under, 31
  limits on student rights under, 11–15
  specificity of government regulation, 75
  wording of, 8
  See also Free speech
Flaherty, Jack, Jr., 131–134
Foreign countries
  cases, 49, 86, 104–105
  cell phone restrictions, 85
  computers provided to students in, 1
  cyberbullying in, 2, 77, 98, 164–165
  Internet addiction, 105
  Internet rights in, 1
  Internet usage by young people in, 1
  laws, 1, 21
France, 1
Frankfurter, Felix, 11
Fraser (1986)
  case and decision, 12–13
  Jill Snyder and, 77
  Justin Layshock and, 47
  Nick Emmett and, 111
Fraser, Matthew, 13
Frederick, Joseph, case of (2007), 14–15
Free speech
  fear and, 126
  First Amendment protection of, 8, 31
  Supreme Court rulings about Internet and, 15
  teaching civil discourse and, 67
  unpopular, 41, 96, 97
  Web site about right to, 69
Fulmer, Kathleen, 28–30

G

Gagnon, Nicholas, 57
Gang posturing, 98
Garrido v. Krasnasky (Vermont, 2008), 66
Germany, 49
Gillan, Megan, 165
Glover, Logan, 85–86
Gobert, Shawn, 54, 55
Goldsmith, Lloyd, Jr., 143
Goldsmith and Morgan v. Brookwood High School
  (Georgia, 2003), 143
Grand jury, defined, 177
Graphic arts, 112, 113, 115–118, 119–120
Great Britain, 1
Greenthal, Jonah, 151
Gregory Requa v. Kent School District (Washington,
  2007), 81–84
Grogan, Holly, 165

H

Hacking, 147–150, 151–157
Hailee Wiggins-Ketchum v. Corona del Mar High School
  (California, 2009), 168
Halligan, Ryan Patrick, 166
Happy slapping, 127–128, 177
Harassment
  defined, 177
  intent and, 53–56, 57
  tips for dealing with (Web site), 92
Harris, Tony, 134
Hate crimes, 99, 106
Hate speech
  about, 30
  defined, 177
  state case, 31
Hauser, Jessica, 85–86
Hazelwood (1988), 13–14, 111
Help lines, x, 43, 100
  dealing with cyberbullying, 92, 169
  reporting online sexual exploitation, 79
  safe email usage, 39
  safe instant messaging, 120
  safe Internet usage, 60, 145
  safety on social networking sites, 51, 79
Holly, Josh, 152–153

Index 191

Houghton, Keeley, 105–106
Hung jury, defined, 177

I

Imel v. Charles A. Beard School (Indiana, 2006), 113
I.M.L. v. State of Utah (2002), 71–74, 75
Incorrigible, defined, 177
Indictment, defined, 177
In re Gault, 11
Instant messaging (IM), 115–117, 118, 120, 177
International Safer Internet Day (Web site), 21
Internet
  access as right, 1
  addiction, 104–105
  benefits of, 104
  colleges and, 59, 67
  effect on teens of, 2, 4–5, 116
  extent of usage, 1, 38
  name searches on, 59, 77
  privacy on, 16–17, 135
  safety tips for using, 43, 60, 107, 145
  school use policies, 93–96
  Supreme Court rulings about free speech on, 15
  writing skills development and, 48
Interstate Communications Law (1948), 18
In the Matter of Abraham Biggs (Florida, 2008), 162
In the Matter of Brian Conradt (Indiana, 1999), 106–107
In the Matter of J. M. (Arkansas, 2000), 119
In the Matter of Jeffrey Johnston (Florida, 2005), 164–165
In the Matter of Rachael Neblett (Kentucky, 2006), 163
In the Matter of Ricky Alatorre (Indiana, 2008), 167
In the Matter of Ryan Patrick Halligan (Vermont, 2003), 166
In the Matter of Seven Girls (Indiana, 2008), 128
In the Matter of Singh (Wisconsin, 2003), 113
In the Matter of Texting at Monarch High (Colorado, 2007), 67–68
In the Matter of Three Branden River High Students (Florida, 2008), 118–119
In the Matter of 21 Students (California, 2006), 106
Israel, 1

J

Jack Flaherty Jr. v. Keystone Oaks School District (Pennsylvania, 2003), 131–134
Jackson, Mandi, 58–59
Japan, 85, 165
Jefferson, Thomas, 72
Jill Snyder v. Blue Mountain School District (Pennsylvania, 2008), 77
John Doe, through next friend Laura Cook v. R.C., A.G., K.Z., and M.S. (Illinois, 2009), 76
Johnston, Jeffrey, 164–165
Jon Coy v. Canton City Schools (Ohio, 2002), 93–96
Joshua Mahaffey v. Waterford School District (Michigan, 2002), 101–104

J.S. Bethlehem v. Area School District (Pennsylvania, 2002), 27–30, 32
Judicial system
  federal and state, 9
  researching opinions, 121, 172–173
  responsibility to First Amendment, 171
  rights of young people in, 11
  rulings and particular courts, 56
  treatment as adult in, 99, 123–126, 127–128
Justin Boucher v. School District of Greenfield (Wisconsin, 1998), 147–150
Justin Layshock v. Hermitage School District (Pennsylvania, 2007), 45–48
Juvenile courts, 10, 129

K

Karl Beidler v. North Thurston School District (Washington, 2000), 32–33
Kartsotis, Thomas, 28–30
Katherine Evans v. Peter Bayer, 76
Keeley Houghton, Worcester Crown Court (England, 2009), 105–106
Kernell, David C., 154
Khan, Omar, 154–155
Kilpatrick, Kwame, 39
Kim, Paul, 135–136
King, Larry, 99
Kuhl, Ryan, 40

L

Lake, Ian Michael, 71–75
Larson, Kelsey, 143
Larson v. Birdville High School (Texas, 2005), 143
Lathouwer, Ryan, 143–144
Latour, Antony, 112
Laws
  ex post facto, 159
  federal, 18
  finding, 17
  foreign, 1, 21
  state, 18–21
Layshock, Justin, 45–49
Leeson, Sam, 164–165
Legal research, 121, 172–173
Lehnis, Dave, 32
Lewdness
  cell phone video clips, 81–87
  in schools, 12–13
  sexting, 88–91
  on Web sites, 112, 135–136
Libel, 71–78, 86, 178
Lindsay, Victoria, 127–128
Location, off-campus *vs.* on-campus
  of comments posted, 134
  disruption of school and, 133
  importance of, 27–33
  purpose of communication and, 61–65
  rights and, 15

school codes of conduct and, 126–127
school responsibility, 10
use of school property and, 93–96
of Web site creation, 27–30, 101–014, 135–136
Logan, Jessica, 89–90
Logan Glover v. Lafayette High School (Missouri, 2008), 85–86
Lopez, Maria Amelia, 66

M

Machado, Richard, 31
Madison, James, 96
Mahaffey, Joshua, 101–104
Make a Difference for Kids (Web site), 163
McEvoy, Jonathan, 57
McGonigle, James, 77
McInerney, Brandon, 99
Megan Meier Cyberbullying Prevention Act (2008), 18
Meier, Megan, 18, 157–160
Metallo, John, 38–39
Miller, Marissa, 87
Miller v. Skumanick (Pennsylvania, 2009), 87
Minors. *See* Young people
Misdemeanor, defined, 178
Mitchell, Dustin, 126–127
Moore, Emily, 105–106
Morgan, Edward, 143
Mortimer, Joshua, 123–126
Movies, 113
Murakowski, Maciej, 112
Murakowski v. University of Delaware (Delaware, 2008), 112
Music, 112–113, 118–119
Muss, Carlson, 33
Muss v. Beaverton School District (Oregon, 2003), 33
MySpace, 50–51
   See also Social networking sites

N

NAACP v. Button (1963), 75
Neal, Justin, 40
Neblett, Rachael, 163
Negligence, defined, 178
New Jersey v. T.L.O. (1985), 150
Nick Emmett v. Kent School District (Washington, 2000), 109–111
Nominal damages, defined, 178

O

O'Brien, Sean, 42
Off-campus *vs.* on-campus. *See* Location, off-campus *vs.* on-campus

Offensive speech, 61–65
   abusive, 33, 35–38
   lewd
      A.B., 53–56
      Fraser, 12–13
      Jill Snyder, 77
      Justin Layshock, 45–48
      In the Matter of Singh, 113
      Murakowski, 112
      Thomas, 58
   location of access of, 93–96
   political content, 53–56, 97
   sexual content, 135–136
Olmstead v. United States (1928), 68
Online message boards, 132–135

P

Paul, Zachariah, 35–38, 39
Petty offense, defined, 178
Phelps, Sarah, 76
Political speech, protection of, 53–56, 96, 97
Principals. *See* School personnel
Privacy
   of email, 35–39
   on Internet, 16–17, 135
   public schools and, 58–59
   right to, 68, 179
   texting/sexting and, 67–68, 91
   Web site about right to, 69
   at workplace, 67
   of young people, 54, 64
Private schools, 13
Probable cause, defined, 179
Probation, defined, 179
Protecting Children in the 21st Century Act (2008), 18
Public schools
   disruption of functioning of
      Aaron Wisniewski, 115–117
      Avery Doninger, 61–65
      Dresser case, 10
      Gregory Requa, 81–84
      Jack Flaherty, 131–134
      Joshua Mahaffey, 101–104
      Justin Boucher, 147–150
      Justin Laycock, 45–48
      In the Matter of 21 Students, 106
      New Jersey, 150
      Ryan Kuhl, 40
      Tinker, 11–12
      Zachariah Paul, 37, 38
   invasion of students' privacy by, 58–59
   policies/codes of conduct
      AUPs, 94–96, 136, 149
      cell phones, 68
      legal requirements for cyberbullying, 17
      location of incident, 126–127
      vagueness of, 131–134
      written materials, 58

publications, 13–14, 147–150
    student rights in private vs., 13
    use of lewd language in, 12–13
    values taught in, 67, 150
    See also School personnel
Punitive damages, defined, 179
Purtell v. Mason (Illinois, 2008), 31

Q/R

Quon v. Arch Wireless Operating Co. (California, 2008), 67
Reasonable doubt, defined, 179
Red Lake, Minnesota, 127
Requa, Gregory, 81–84
Restitution, defined, 179
Rights of minority, 96
"Rules of the St. Croix Jail" (Dresser), 10
Ryan Dwyer v. Oceanport School District (New Jersey, 2005), 139–142
Ryan Kuhl v. Greenwood School District (Arkansas, 2005), 40

S

Sacco, Nicola, 148
Sanford, Mark, 39
Schick, Cozy Lynn, 153–154
Schlicker, Hughstan, 105
School personnel
    cyberbullying in foreign countries of, 77, 119
    derogatory comments about, 33, 35–38, 40–42, 53–56
    harassment of, 32–33, 76–77, 86–87
    lewd video clips of, 81–85
    libeling, 71–74
    threats against, 27–30, 106–107, 143
    unauthorized video clips of, 81–86
Schools, 13
    See also Public schools; School personnel
Schreiber, Benjamin, 49–50
Sean O'Brien v. Westlake Board of Education (Ohio, 1998), 42
Sexting, 87, 88–91
Sexual crimes online, 50, 51, 79, 86–91
Siefert, Thomas, 135
Singapore, 2
Singh, Sashwat, 113
Singh, Tanvir, 154–155
Slander, defined, 180
Snyder, Jill, 77
Social networking sites
    benefits of, 48
    derogatory pages on, 53–56
    extent of usage, 50–51
    fake profiles on
        Draker, 49–50
        in foreign countries, 2
        Jill Snyder, 77

John Doe, 76
Justin Layshock, 45–48
In the Matter of Ricky Alatorre, 167
United States v. Lori Drew, 157–160
    gang posturing on, 98
    hacking into, 153–154
    libel and, 75–77
    links to, 81–84
    offensive language on, 58–59
    photos on, 59
    profile privacy, 57
    profile readers, 57
    teen profile statistics, 1
    threats on, 105–106, 118–119, 153–154, 167, 168
    tips for using safely, 51, 59, 60, 79
    violence on, 127–128
Solis, Pete, 50–51
South Korea, 104, 105, 164
State court system, 9, 172–173
State laws, 18–21, 72, 165
State of Texas v. Solis (Texas, 2006), 50
State v. Alpert (Florida, 2008), 87
State v. Brittini Hardcastle and four others (Florida, 2008), 127–128
State v. Dougherty (Iowa, 2008), 86–87
State v. Joshua Mortimer (North Carolina, 2001), 123–126
State v. Machado (California, 1998), 31
State v. McEvoy and Gagnon (Colorado, 2007), 57
State v. McInerney (California, 2008), 99
State v. Nicole Williams (Missouri, 2008), 162
State v. Omar Khan and Tanvir Singh (California, 2008), 154–155
State v. Schick (Minnesota, 2007), 153–154
Statute of limitations, defined, 180
Stop Cyberbullying Pledge, 161
Suicides, 20, 89–90, 157–160, 162–166
Sullivan, Dan, 58
Supreme Court, 15, 121, 172–173
    See also specific cases
Swidler, Justin, 28–30, 32

T

Taiwan, 104
Teachers. *See* School personnel
Teens
    effect of Internet on, 2, 4–5
    email and Internet usage statistics, 38
    IM and texting statistics, 118
    Internet addiction statistics, 104–105
    issues discussed on MySpace, 57
    reading and writing blogs statistics, 66
Terminiello v. City of Chicago (1949), 40
Text messages
    benefits of, 66–67
    by politicians, 39
    potential of, 68
    privacy of, 67–68
    sexual, 88–91

threats, 162
usage statistics, 118
to wrong number, 38
Thomas, Clarence, 15
Thomas, Donna, 58
Thomas Siefert v. Lancaster High School (Ohio, 2003), 135
Thomas v. Granville Central School District (New York, 1979), 58
Threats
    Columbine High School and, 124–127
    elements of proof, 124
    email, 31, 163
    icons, 115–117
    musical, 112–113, 118–119
    on social networking sites, 105–106, 167, 168
    state cases, 31, 33
    text messages, 162
    true, defined, 103, 180
    video, 113, 119–120, 168
    on Web sites, 27–30, 101–104, 106–107, 109–111, 143
Tinker (1969)
    case and decision, 11–12, 126
    Jack Flaherty Jr. and, 133
    Justin Boucher and, 149
    Justin Laycock and, 47
    Nick Emmett and, 111
    Zachariah Paul and, 37
Tinker siblings, 11–12
Trial courts, 9
Trosch, Eric, 46–48
True threats, defined, 103, 180

U/V

United States v. David Kernell (Tennessee, 2008), 154
United States v. Lori Drew (California, 2008), 157–160
Uruguay, 1
Vanzetti, Bartolomeo, 148
Vesikko (Finland, 2007), 86
Video clips
    disruption of functioning of classes, 81–84, 85–86
    of happy slapping, 127–128
    lewd, 81–84c, 86–87
    sexting, 86–91
    of suicide, 162
    threats, 119–120, 168
    unauthorized of school personnel, 85–86
Video Threats at Agawam Junior High (Massachusetts, 2008), 119–120
Violence, 127–128
    See also Threats
Voltaire, 96

W

Walker, Owen Thor, 152
Web sites
    intent and, 109–111
    location of creation of, 27–30, 135–136
    responsibility for content on, 139–142, 143–144
    threats on, 27–30, 101–104, 106–107, 109–111, 143
Weigman, Matthew, 153
Weiss, Jeffrey James, 127
White hat hackers, 151, 152
Whitney v. California (1927), 126
Wiggins-Ketchum, Hallie, 168
Williams, Nicole, 162
Winfrey, Oprah, 16
Wisniewski, Aaron, 115–117, 118
Witsell, Hope, 91
Wolfe, Billy, 167
Workplace issues, 67, 134–135
Written expression
    banners, 14–15
    benefits of digital, 68
    distribution of, 58
    extent allowed in public schools of, 13–14
    newspapers, 58
    offline, 119
    potential of students, 68
    unofficial school home page, 109–111

Y/Z

Young people
    age minimum on social networking sites, 50–51
    Internet usage statistics, 1
    privacy of, 54, 64
    prosecuted as adults, 99, 123–126, 127–128
    responsibility for education of, 14
    rights of, 10–15
    victims of cyberbullies statistics, xi, 3
    See also Teens
YouTube, blockage of offensive materials, 120
Zachariah Paul v. Franklin Regional School District (Pennsylvania, 2001), 35–38

About the Author

Thomas A. Jacobs, J.D., was an Arizona Assistant Attorney General from 1972–1985, where he practiced criminal and child welfare law. He was appointed to the Maricopa County Superior Court in 1985, where he served as a judge pro tem and commissioner in the juvenile and family courts until his retirement in 2008. He also taught juvenile law for 10 years as an adjunct professor at the Arizona State University School of Social Work. He continues to write for teens, lawyers, and judges.

Visit his Web site, AsktheJudge.info, for free interactive educational tools that provide current information regarding laws, court decisions, and national news affecting teens. It's the only site of its kind to provide legal questions and answers for teens and parents with the unique ability to interact with Judge Jacobs and other teens.

Do you have lots of ideas and opinions? Have you ever seen a book or website and thought, "I'd do that differently"?

Then we want to hear from you! We're looking for teens to be part of the **Free Spirit Teen Advisory Council.** You'll help us keep our books and other products current and relevant by letting us know what you think about things like design, art, and content.

Go to www.freespirit.com/teens to learn more and get an application.

Other Teen Books from Free Spirit

They Broke the Law—You Be the Judge
True Cases of Teen Crime
by Thomas A. Jacobs, J.D.
This book invites teens to preside over a variety of real-life cases, to learn each teen's background, the relevant facts, and the sentencing options available. After deciding on a sentence, they find out what really happened—and where each offender is today. For ages 12 & up. *224 pp.; paperback; 6" x 9"*

What Are My Rights?
Q&A About Teens and the Law (Revised and Updated 3rd Edition)
by Thomas A. Jacobs, J.D.
Teens often have questions about the law, but they don't always know where to turn for answers. Judge Jacobs uses a straightforward "just the facts" tone and draws on examples from real-life court cases involving young people to help teens learn about the laws that affect them, appreciate their rights, and consider their responsibilities.
For ages 12 & up. *224 pp.; paperback; 6" x 9"*

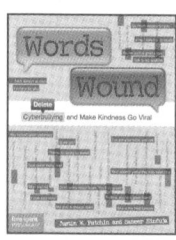

Words Wound
Delete Cyberbullying and Make Kindness Go Viral
by Justin W. Patchin, Ph.D., and Sameer Hinduja, Ph.D.
Vicious words and damaging photos exchanged through texts, email, or social media can result in humiliation, broken friendships, punishment at school, and even legal prosecution. Written by experts in cyberbullying prevention, this book provides strategies for teens dealing with cyberbullying as well as for those who have taken part in bullying others. For ages 13 & up.
200 pp.; paperback; 2-color; 6" x 7½"

Interested in purchasing multiple quantities and receiving volume discounts?
Contact edsales@freespirit.com or call 1.800.735.7323 and ask for Education Sales.

Many Free Spirit authors are available for speaking engagements, workshops, and keynotes.
Contact speakers@freespirit.com or call 1.800.735.7323.

For pricing information, to place an order, or to request a free catalog, contact:

Free Spirit Publishing Inc.
217 Fifth Avenue North • Suite 200 • Minneapolis, MN 55401-1299
toll-free 800.735.7323 • local 612.338.2068 • fax 612.337.5050
help4kids@freespirit.com • www.freespirit.com

WITHDRAWN
KELLY LIBRARY
EMORY & HENRY COLLEGE
EMORY VA 24327